MznLnx

Missing Links Exam Preps

Exam Prep for

Macroeconomics Explore and Apply

Ayers, Collinge, 1st Edition

The MznLnx Exam Prep is your link from the texbook and lecture to your exams.
The MznLnx Exam Preps are unauthorized and comprehensive reviews of your textbooks.

All material provided by MznLnx and Rico Publications (c) 2010
Textbook publishers and textbook authors do not particpate in or contribute to these reviews.

MznLnx

Rico
Publications

Exam Prep for Macroeconomics Explore and Apply
1st Edition
Ayers, Collinge

Publisher: Raymond Houge
Assistant Editor: Michael Rouger
Text and Cover Designer: Lisa Buckner
Marketing Manager: Sara Swagger
Project Manager, Editorial Production: Jerry Emerson
Art Director: Vernon Lowerui

Product Manager: Dave Mason
Editorial Assitant: Rachel Guzmanji
Pedagogy: Debra Long
Cover Image: Jim Reed/Getty Images
Text and Cover Printer: City Printing, Inc.
Compositor: Media Mix, Inc.

(c) 2010 Rico Publications
ALL RIGHTS RESERVED. No part of this work covered by the copyright may be reproduced or used in any form or by an means--graphic, electronic, or mechanical, including photocopying, recording, taping, Web distribution, information storage, and retrieval systems, or in any other manner--without the written permission of the publisher.

Printed in the United States
ISBN:

For more information about our products, contact us at:
Dave.Mason@RicoPublications.com

For permission to use material from this text or product, submit a request online to:
Dave.Mason@RicoPublications.com

Contents

CHAPTER 1
The Economic Perspective — 1

CHAPTER 2
Production and Trade — 9

CHAPTER 3
Demand and Supply — 13

CHAPTER 4
The Power of Prices — 16

CHAPTER 5
Measuring National Output — 23

CHAPTER 6
Unemployment — 37

CHAPTER 7
Inflation — 40

CHAPTER 8
A Framework for Macroeconomic Analysis — 48

CHAPTER 9
Fiscal Policy and Short-Run Instability — 54

CHAPTER 10
Aggregate Expenditures — 61

CHAPTER 11
Fiscal Policy in Action — 67

CHAPTER 12
Economic Growth — 74

CHAPTER 13
Money, Banking, and the Federal Reserve — 78

CHAPTER 14
Monetary Policy and Price Stability — 90

CHAPTER 15
Into the International Marketplace — 98

CHAPTER 16
Policy Toward Trade — 105

CHAPTER 17
Economic Development — 111

ANSWER KEY — 116

TO THE STUDENT

COMPREHENSIVE

The *MznLnx* Exam Prep series is designed to help you pass your exams. Editors at MznLnx review your textbooks and then prepare these practice exams to help you master the textbook material. Unlike study guides, workbooks, and practice tests provided by the texbook publisher and textbook authors, *MznLnx* gives you **all** of the material in each chapter in exam form, not just samples, so you can be sure to nail your exam.

MECHANICAL

The MznLnx Exam Prep series creates exams that will help you learn the subject matter as well as test you on your understanding. Each question is designed to help you master the concept. Just working through the exams, you gain an understanding of the subject--its a simple mechanical process that produces success.

INTEGRATED STUDY GUIDE AND REVIEW

MznLnx is not just a set of exams designed to test you, its also a comprehensive review of the subject content. Each exam question is also a review of the concept, making sure that you will get the answer correct without having to go to other sources of material. You learn as you go! Its the easiest way to pass an exam.

HUMOR

Studying can be tedious and dry. MznLnx's instructional design includes moderate humor within the exam questions on occassion, to break the tedium and revitalize the brain

Chapter 1. The Economic Perspective 1

1. _____ is a broad label that refers to any individuals or households that use goods and services generated within the economy. The concept of a _____ is used in different contexts, so that the usage and significance of the term may vary.

Typically when business people and economists talk of _____s they are talking about person as _____, an aggregated commodity item with little individuality other than that expressed in the buy/not-buy decision.

   a. 100-year flood
   c. 130-30 fund
   b. 1921 recession
   d. Consumer

2. _____s is the social science that studies the production, distribution, and consumption of goods and services. The term _____s comes from the Ancient Greek oá¼°κονομῖα from oá¼¶κος (oikos, 'house') + vÏŒμος (nomos, 'custom' or 'law'), hence 'rules of the house(hold)'. Current _____ models developed out of the broader field of political economy in the late 19th century, owing to a desire to use an empirical approach more akin to the physical sciences.
   a. Energy economics
   c. Economic
   b. Opportunity cost
   d. Inflation

3. In economics and finance, _____ is the change in total cost that arises when the quantity produced changes by one unit. It is the cost of producing one more unit of a good. Mathematically, the _____ function is expressed as the first derivative of the total cost (TC) function with respect to quantity (Q.)
   a. Variable cost
   c. Marginal cost
   b. Quality costs
   d. Khozraschyot

4. _____ is used to assign the available resources in an economic way. It is part of resource management.

In strategic planning,is a plan for using available resources, for example human resources, especially in the near term, to achieve goals for the future.

   a. 1921 recession
   c. 130-30 fund
   b. 100-year flood
   d. Resource allocation

5. _____ is an online peer-reviewed magazine published by the Agricultural ' Applied Economics Association (AAEA) for readers interested in the policy and management of agriculture, the food industry, natural resources, rural communities, and the environment. _____ is published quarterly and is available free online. It is currently one of three outreach products offered by AAEA, along with the more timely Policy Issues and the forthcoming Shared Materials section of the AAEA Web site.
   a. 130-30 fund
   c. 1921 recession
   b. Choices
   d. 100-year flood

6. The _____ or gross domestic income (GDI), a basic measure of an economy's economic performance, is the market value of all final goods and services produced within the borders of a nation in a year. _____ can be defined in three ways, all of which are conceptually identical. First, it is equal to the total expenditures for all final goods and services produced within the country in a stipulated period of time (usually a 365-day year.)
   a. Countercyclical
   c. Monopolistic competition
   b. Market structure
   d. Gross domestic product

Chapter 1. The Economic Perspective

7. In economics and sociology, an _____ is any factor (financial or non-financial) that enables or motivates a particular course of action, or counts as a reason for preferring one choice to the alternatives. It is an expectation that encourages people to behave in a certain way. Since human beings are purposeful creatures, the study of _____ structures is central to the study of all economic activity (both in terms of individual decision-making and in terms of co-operation and competition within a larger institutional structure.)

   a. Economic reform
   b. Isocost
   c. Epstein-Zin preferences
   d. Incentive

8. _____, 1st Baron Keynes was a renowned economist from Britain whose many ideas on economic and political theories as well as on many governments' monetary policies influenced America. He advocated a government that played an active role in the lives of people regarding business, economy, etc. In this role, the government would use fiscal measures to reduce the consequences of recessions, economic depressions and booms.

   a. Adolf Hitler
   b. Adam Smith
   c. Adolph Fischer
   d. John Maynard Keynes

9. _____ and Keynesian Theory) is a macroeconomic theory based on the ideas of 20th-century British economist John Maynard Keynes. _____ argues that private sector decisions sometimes lead to inefficient macroeconomic outcomes and therefore advocates active policy responses by the public sector, including monetary policy actions by the central bank and fiscal policy actions by the government to stabilize output over the business cycle.

The theories forming the basis of _____ were first presented in The General Theory of Employment, Interest and Money, published in 1936.

   a. Rational choice theory
   b. Market failure
   c. Keynesian economics
   d. Deflation

10. _____ is a branch of economics that deals with the performance, structure, and behavior of a national or regional economy as a whole. Along with microeconomics, _____ is one of the two most general fields in economics. It is the study of the behavior and decision-making of entire economies.

   a. Nominal value
   b. Macroeconomics
   c. Tobit model
   d. New Trade Theory

11. _____ is an economic concept with commonplace familiarity. It is the price that a good or service is offered at, or will fetch, in the marketplace. It is of interest mainly in the study of microeconomics.

   a. Market price
   b. Noisy market hypothesis
   c. Market anomaly
   d. Paper trading

12. _____ is a branch of economics that studies how individuals, households and firms and some states make decisions to allocate limited resources, typically in markets where goods or services are being bought and sold. _____ examines how these decisions and behaviours affect the supply and demand for goods and services, which determines prices; and how prices, in turn, determine the supply and demand of goods and services.

Whereas macroeconomics involves the 'sum total of economic activity, dealing with the issues of growth, inflation and unemployment, and with national economic policies relating to these issues' and the effects of government actions on them.

Chapter 1. The Economic Perspective

a. New Keynesian economics   b. Microeconomics
c. Recession   d. Countercyclical

13. _____ in economics and business is the result of an exchange and from that trade we assign a numerical monetary value to a good, service or asset. If Alice trades Bob 4 apples for an orange, the _____ of an orange is 4 apples. Inversely, the _____ of an apple is 1/4 oranges.
   a. Price book   b. Premium pricing
   c. Price   d. Price war

14. An _____ or Å"conomic system is a system that involves the production, distribution and consumption of goods and services between the entities in a particular society. It is the method used by society to produce and distribute goods and services. The _____ is composed of people and institutions, including their relationships to productive resources, such as through the convention of property.
   a. Indicative planning   b. Economic system
   c. Intention economy   d. Information economy

15. A _____ is a theoretical term that economists use to describe a market which is free from government intervention (i.e. no regulation, no subsidization, no single monetary system and no governmental monopolies.) In a _____, property rights are voluntarily exchanged at a price arranged solely by the mutual consent of sellers and buyers. By definition, buyers and sellers do not coerce each other, in the sense that they obtain each other's property without the use of physical force, threat of physical force, or fraud, nor is the coerced by a third party (such as by government via transfer payments) and they engage in trade simply because they both consent and believe that it is a good enough choice.
   a. Leninism   b. Free market
   c. Third camp   d. Delegation

16. _____ is a situation in which the limited resources of a firm are allocated in accordance with the wishes of consumers. An allocatively efficient economy produces an 'optimal mix' of commodities. A firm is allocatively efficient when its price is equal to its marginal costs (that is, P = MC) in a perfect market.
   a. ACEA agreement   b. Allocative efficiency
   c. ACCRA Cost of Living Index   d. Economic efficiency

17. _____ is used to refer to a number of related concepts. It is the using resources in such a way as to maximize the production of goods and services. A system can be called economically efficient if:

- No one can be made better off without making someone else worse off.
- More output cannot be obtained without increasing the amount of inputs.
- Production proceeds at the lowest possible per-unit cost.

These definitions of efficiency are not equivalent, but they are all encompassed by the idea that nothing more can be achieved given the resources available.

An economic system is more efficient if it can provide more goods and services for society without using more resources.

a. ACCRA Cost of Living Index
b. ACEA agreement
c. Efficient contract theory
d. Economic efficiency

18. _____ is the concept or idea of fairness in economics, particularly as to taxation or welfare economics.

In welfare economics, _____ may be distinguished from economic efficiency in overall evaluation of social welfare. Although '_____' has broader uses, it may be posed as a counterpart to economic inequality in yielding a 'good' distribution of welfare.

a. ACCRA Cost of Living Index
b. ACEA agreement
c. AD-IA Model
d. Equity

19. _____ was a survey conducted by the U.S. Department of Justice to gauge the prevalence of alcohol and illegal drug use among prior arrestees. It was a reformulation of the prior Drug Use Forecasting (DUF) program, focused on five drugs in particular: cocaine, marijuana, methamphetamine, opiates, and PCP.

Participants were randomly selected from arrest records in major metropolitan areas; because no personally identifying information is taken from each record chosen, the resulting data can be correlated to arrest rates, but not to the total population of persons charged.

a. ACCRA Cost of Living Index
b. ACEA agreement
c. Arrestee Drug Abuse Monitoring
d. AD-IA Model

20. In economics, the _____ is the term economists use to describe the self-regulating nature of the marketplace. The _____ is a metaphor coined by the economist Adam Smith in The Wealth of Nations.

Adam Smith mentions the metaphor in Book IV of The Wealth of Nations, arguing that people in any society will certainly employ their capital in foreign trading only if the profits available by that method far exceed those available locally, and that in such a case it is better for society as a whole if they so did.

a. Invisible hand
b. AD-IA Model
c. ACCRA Cost of Living Index
d. ACEA agreement

21. _____ is the controlled distribution of resources and scarce goods or services. _____ controls the size of the ration, one's allotted portion of the resources being distributed on a particular day or at a particular time.

In economics, it is often common to use the word '_____' to refer to one of the roles that prices play in markets, while _____ is called 'non-price _____.' Using prices to ration means that those with the most money (or other assets) and who want a product the most are first to receive it.

a. 130-30 fund
b. 100-year flood
c. 1921 recession
d. Rationing

Chapter 1. The Economic Perspective

22. _____ was a Scottish moral philosopher and a pioneer of political economy. One of the key figures of the Scottish Enlightenment, Smith is the author of The Theory of Moral Sentiments and An Inquiry into the Nature and Causes of the Wealth of Nations. The latter, usually abbreviated as The Wealth of Nations, is considered his magnum opus and the first modern work of economics.
    a. Adolph Fischer
    b. Alan Greenspan
    c. Adam Smith
    d. Adolf Hitler

23. An Inquiry into the Nature and Causes of the _____ is the magnum opus of the Scottish economist Adam Smith. It is a clearly written account of economics at the dawn of the Industrial Revolution, as well as a rhetorical piece written for the generally educated individual of the 18th century - advocating a free market economy as more productive and more beneficial to society.

    The work is credited as a watershed in history and economics due to its comprehensive, largely accurate characterization of economic mechanisms that survive in modern economics; and also for its effective use of rhetorical technique, including structuring the work to contrast real world examples of free and fettered markets.
    a. The Bell Curve
    b. The Rise and Fall of the Great Powers
    c. Black Book of Communism
    d. Wealth of Nations

24. In economics, a _____ exists when the production or use of goods and services by the market is not efficient. That is, there exists another outcome where all involved can be made better off. _____s can be viewed as scenarios where individuals' pursuit of pure self-interest leads to results that are not efficient - that can be improved upon from the societal point-of-view.
    a. Fixed exchange rate
    b. Market failure
    c. General equilibrium
    d. Financial economics

25. In economics, a _____ is any economic system that effects its distribution of goods and services with prices and employing any form of money or debt tokens. Except for possible remote and primitive communities, all modern societies use _____s to allocate resources. However, _____s are not used for all resource allocation decisions today.
    a. Family economy
    b. Hanseatic League
    c. Neomercantilism
    d. Price system

26. In economics, an _____ is any good or commodity, transported from one country to another country in a legitimate fashion, typically for use in trade. _____ goods or services are provided to foreign consumers by domestic producers. _____ is an important part of international trade.
    a. ACCRA Cost of Living Index
    b. Export
    c. AD-IA Model
    d. ACEA agreement

27. A _____ arises when one infers that something is true of the whole from the fact that it is true of some part of the whole (or even of every proper part.) For example: 'This fragment of metal cannot be broken with a hammer, therefore the machine of which it is a part cannot be broken with a hammer.' This is clearly fallacious, because many machines can be broken into their constituent parts without any of those parts being breakable.

    This fallacy is often confused with the fallacy of hasty generalization, in which an unwarranted inference is made from a statement about a sample to a statement about the population from which it is drawn.

Chapter 1. The Economic Perspective

a. 100-year flood
b. 1921 recession
c. 130-30 fund
d. Fallacy of composition

28. _____ originally was the term for studying production, buying and selling, and their relations with law, custom, and government. _____ originated in moral philosophy. It developed in the 18th century as the study of the economies of states -- polities, hence _____.

a. Productive and unproductive labour
b. Political economy
c. Dirigisme
d. Geoeconomics

29. _____ is the branch of economics that incorporates value judgments (that is, normative judgements) about what the economy ought to be like or what particular policy actions ought to be recommended to achieve a desirable goal. _____ looks at the desirability of certain aspects of the economy. It underlies expressions of support for particular economic policies.

a. Broad money
b. Double bottom line
c. Nanoeconomics
d. Normative economics

30. _____ is the branch of economics that concerns the description and explanation of economic phenomena (Wong, 1987, p. 920.) It focuses on facts and cause-and-effect relationships and includes the development and testing of economics theories.

a. Regulatory economics
b. 130-30 fund
c. Positive economics
d. 100-year flood

31. Cä"terä«s paribus is a Latin phrase, literally translated as 'with other things the same.' It is commonly rendered in English as 'all other things being equal.' A prediction, or a statement about causal or logical connections between two states of affairs, is qualified by _____ in order to acknowledge, and to rule out, the possibility of other factors which could override the relationship between the antecedent and the consequent.

A _____ assumption is often fundamental to the predictive purpose of scientific inquiry. In order to formulate scientific laws, it is usually necessary to rule out factors which interfere with examining a specific causal relationship.

a. Friedman-Savage utility function
b. Capital outflow
c. Dematerialization
d. Ceteris paribus

32. _____ or Equalism is a political doctrine that holds that all people should be treated as equals and have the same political, economic, social, and civil rights. Generally it applies to being held equal under the law and society at large. In actual practice, one may be considered an egalitarian in most areas listed below, even if not subscribing to equality in every possible area of individual difference.

a. ACEA agreement
b. AD-IA Model
c. ACCRA Cost of Living Index
d. Egalitarianism

33.

_____ was a German philosopher, political economist, historian, political theorist, sociologist, communist and revolutionary credited as the founder of communism.

Chapter 1. The Economic Perspective 7

Marx summarized his approach to history and politics in the opening line of the first chapter of The Communist Manifesto : e;The history of all hitherto existing society is the history of class struggles.e; Marx argued that capitalism, like previous socioeconomic systems, will produce internal tensions which will lead to its destruction. Just as capitalism replaced feudalism, socialism will in its turn replace capitalism and lead to a stateless, classless society which will emerge after a transitional period, the 'dictatorship of the proletariat'.

- a. Adam Smith
- b. Neo-Gramscianism
- c. Marxism
- d. Karl Heinrich Marx

34. A _____ is an economy based on the division of labor in which the prices of goods and services are determined in a free price system set by supply and demand. This is often contrasted with a planned economy, in which a central government determines the price of goods and services using a fixed price system. Market economies are contrasted with mixed economy where the price system is not entirely free but under some government control that is not extensive enough to constitute a planned economy.
- a. Network Economy
- b. Nutritional Economics
- c. Commons-based peer production
- d. Market economy

35. An inverse or negative relationship is a mathematical relationship in which one variable, say y, decreases as another, say x, increases. For a linear (straight-line) relation, this can be expressed as y = a-bx, where -b is a constant value less than zero and a is a constant. For example, there is an _____ between education and unemployment -- that is, as education increases, the rate of unemployment decreases.
- a. Inverse relationship
- b. AD-IA Model
- c. ACEA agreement
- d. ACCRA Cost of Living Index

36. _____ or cross section (of a study population) in statistics and econometrics is a type of one-dimensional data set. _____ refers to data collected by observing many subjects (such as individuals, firms or countries/regions) at the same point of time, or without regard to differences in time. Analysis of _____ usually consists of comparing the differences among the subjects.
- a. 100-year flood
- b. 130-30 fund
- c. 1921 recession
- d. Cross-sectional data

37. In mathematics, a _____ system is a system which is not linear, that is, a system which does not satisfy the superposition principle, or whose output is not proportional to its input. Less technically, a _____ system is any problem where the variable(s) to be solved for cannot be written as a linear combination of independent components. A nonhomogeneous system, which is linear apart from the presence of a function of the independent variables, is _____ according to a strict definition, but such systems are usually studied alongside linear systems, because they can be transformed to a linear system of multiple variables.
- a. Nonlinear system
- b. 100-year flood
- c. 130-30 fund
- d. Nonlinear

38. _____ are usually numerical time-series, i.e., sets of data (covering periods of time) for part or all of a single economy or the international economy. When they are time-series the data sets are usually monthly but can be quarterly and annual. The data may be adjusted in various ways (for ease of further analysis), most commonly adjusted or unadjusted for seasonal fluctuations.

a. ACEA agreement
b. AD-IA Model
c. ACCRA Cost of Living Index
d. Economic data

39. Unemployment occurs when a person is available to work and seeking work but currently without work. The prevalence of unemployment is usually measured using the _____, which is defined as the percentage of those in the labor force who are unemployed. The _____ is also used in economic studies and economic indexes such as the United States' Conference Board's Index of Leading Indicators as a measure of the state of the macroeconomics.
   a. ACCRA Cost of Living Index
   b. AD-IA Model
   c. Unemployment rate
   d. ACEA agreement

Chapter 2. Production and Trade

1. _____ refers to the stock of skills and knowledge embodied in the ability to perform labor so as to produce economic value. It is the skills and knowledge gained by a worker through education and experience. Many early economic theories refer to it simply as labor, one of three factors of production, and consider it to be a fungible resource -- homogeneous and easily interchangeable. Other conceptions of labor dispense with these assumptions.
   - a. Human capital
   - b. Law of increasing costs
   - c. General equilibrium
   - d. Price theory

2. _____ is the term denoting either an entrance or changes which are inserted into a system and which activate/modify a process. It is an abstract concept, used in the modeling, system(s) design and system(s) exploitation. It is usually connected with other terms, e.g., _____ field, _____ variable, _____ parameter, _____ value, _____ signal, _____ device and _____ file.
   - a. ACCRA Cost of Living Index
   - b. ACEA agreement
   - c. AD-IA Model
   - d. Input

3. _____ or economic opportunity loss is the value of the next best alternative foregone as the result of making a decision. _____ analysis is an important part of a company's decision-making processes but is not treated as an actual cost in any financial statement. The next best thing that a person can engage in is referred to as the _____ of doing the best thing and ignoring the next best thing to be done.
   - a. Opportunity cost
   - b. Economic ideology
   - c. Industrial organization
   - d. Economic

4. _____ in economics refers to metrics and measures of output from production processes, per unit of input. Labor _____, for example, is typically measured as a ratio of output per labor-hour, an input. _____ may be conceived of as a metrics of the technical or engineering efficiency of production.
   - a. Piece work
   - b. Production-possibility frontier
   - c. Fordism
   - d. Productivity

5. _____ is used to assign the available resources in an economic way. It is part of resource management. In strategic planning, is a plan for using available resources, for example human resources, especially in the near term, to achieve goals for the future.
   - a. 1921 recession
   - b. 130-30 fund
   - c. 100-year flood
   - d. Resource allocation

6. _____ according to Onuoha (2007) is the practice of starting new organizations or revitalizing mature organizations, particularly new businesses generally in response to identified opportunities. _____ is often a difficult undertaking, as a vast majority of new businesses fail. Entrepreneurial activities are substantially different depending on the type of organization that is being started.
   - a. Entrepreneurship
   - b. ACCRA Cost of Living Index
   - c. Intrapreneurship
   - d. ACEA agreement

7. In general _____ refers to any non-human asset made by humans and then used in production. Often, it refers to economic capital in some ambiguous combination of infrastructural capital and natural capital. As these are combined in process-specific and firm-specific ways that neoclassical macroeconomics does not differentiate at its level of analysis, it is common to refer only to physical vs. human capital and seek so-called 'balanced growth' that develops both in tandem

Such analyses, however, fails to make distinctions considered critical by many modern economists.

a. Linkage principle
b. Factor cost
c. Net domestic product
d. Physical capital

8. In microeconomics, _____ is quite simply the conversion of inputs into outputs. It is an economic process that uses resources to create a good or service that is suitable for exchange. This can include manufacturing, storing, shipping, and packaging.
a. MET
b. Red Guards
c. Solved
d. Production

9. _____ is a situation in which the limited resources of a firm are allocated in accordance with the wishes of consumers. An allocatively efficient economy produces an 'optimal mix' of commodities. A firm is allocatively efficient when its price is equal to its marginal costs (that is, P = MC) in a perfect market.
a. ACCRA Cost of Living Index
b. Allocative efficiency
c. Economic efficiency
d. ACEA agreement

10. In calculus, a function f defined on a subset of the real numbers with real values is called _____, if for all x and y such that x >≤ y one has f(x) >≤ f(y), so f preserves the order. In layman's terms, the sign of the slope is always positive (the curve tending upwards) or zero (i.e., non-decreasing, or asymptotic, or depicted as a horizontal, flat line) Likewise, a function is called monotonically decreasing (non-increasing) if, whenever x >≤ y, then f(x) >≥ f(y), so it reverses the order.
a. 130-30 fund
b. 100-year flood
c. 1921 recession
d. Monotonic

11. _____s is the social science that studies the production, distribution, and consumption of goods and services. The term _____s comes from the Ancient Greek oá¼°κονομῖα from oá¼¶κος (oikos, 'house') + vĺŒμος (nomos, 'custom' or 'law'), hence 'rules of the house(hold)'. Current _____ models developed out of the broader field of political economy in the late 19th century, owing to a desire to use an empirical approach more akin to the physical sciences.
a. Energy economics
b. Opportunity cost
c. Inflation
d. Economic

12. _____ is the increase in the amount of the goods and services produced by an economy over time. It is conventionally measured as the percent rate of increase in real gross domestic product, or real GDP. Growth is usually calculated in real terms, i.e. inflation-adjusted terms, in order to net out the effect of inflation on the price of the goods and services produced.
a. ACEA agreement
b. ACCRA Cost of Living Index
c. Economic growth
d. AD-IA Model

13. _____ in economics and business is the result of an exchange and from that trade we assign a numerical monetary value to a good, service or asset. If Alice trades Bob 4 apples for an orange, the _____ of an orange is 4 apples. Inversely, the _____ of an apple is 1/4 oranges.
a. Price war
b. Price
c. Price book
d. Premium pricing

Chapter 2. Production and Trade

14. _____ is a term used in accounting, economics and finance to spread the cost of an asset over the span of several years.

In simple words we can say that _____ is the reduction in the value of an asset due to usage, passage of time, wear and tear, technological outdating or obsolescence, depletion, inadequacy, rot, rust, decay or other such factors.

In accounting, _____ is a term used to describe any method of attributing the historical or purchase cost of an asset across its useful life, roughly corresponding to normal wear and tear.

   a. Historical cost
   b. Salvage value
   c. Net income per employee
   d. Depreciation

15. _____ is a term that is used to describe the overall process of invention, innovation and diffusion of technology or processes. The term is redundant with technological development, technological achievement, and technological progress. In essence _____ is the invention of a technology (or a process), the continuous process of improving a technology (in which it often becomes cheaper) and its diffusion throughout industry or society.
   a. Technological change
   b. 1921 recession
   c. 100-year flood
   d. 130-30 fund

16. In economics, the term _____ of income or _____ refers to a simple economic model which describes the reciprocal circulation of income between producers and consumers. In the _____ model, the inter-dependent entities of producer and consumer are referred to as 'firms' and 'households' respectively and provide each other with factors in order to facilitate the flow of income. Firms provide consumers with goods and services in exchange for consumer expenditure and 'factors of production' from households.
   a. 100-year flood
   b. 130-30 fund
   c. 1921 recession
   d. Circular flow

17. Bartering is a medium in which goods or services are directly exchanged for other goods and/or services, without the use of money. It can be bilateral or multilateral, and usually exists parallel to monetary systems in most developed countries, though to a very limited extent. _____ usually replaces money as the method of exchange in times of monetary crisis, when the currency is unstable and devalued by hyperinflation.
   a. New Economics Foundation
   b. Meitheal
   c. Community-based economics
   d. Barter

18. In economics, _____ refers to the ability of a party to produce a good or service using fewer real resources than another entity producing the same good or service..A party has an _____ when using the same input as another party, it can produce a greater output. Since _____ is determined by a simple comparison of labor productivities, it is possible for a a party to have no _____ in anything. It can be contrasted with the concept of comparative advantage which refers to the ability to produce a particular good at a lower opportunity cost.
   a. ACCRA Cost of Living Index
   b. Index number
   c. Absolute advantage
   d. International economics

Chapter 2. Production and Trade

19. In economics, _____ refers to the ability of a person or a country to produce a particular good at a lower marginal cost and opportunity cost than another person or country. It is the ability to produce a product most efficiently given all the other products that could be produced. It can be contrasted with absolute advantage which refers to the ability of a person or a country to produce a particular good at a lower absolute cost than another.
    a. Gravity model of trade
    b. Triffin dilemma
    c. Hot money
    d. Comparative advantage

20. _____ is a common concept in economics, and gives rise to derived concepts such as consumer debt. Generally _____ is defined by opposition to production. But the precise definition can vary because different schools of economists define production quite differently.
    a. Federal Reserve Bank Notes
    b. Foreclosure data providers
    c. Cash or share options
    d. Consumption

21. In economics, an _____ is any good or commodity, transported from one country to another country in a legitimate fashion, typically for use in trade. _____ goods or services are provided to foreign consumers by domestic producers. _____ is an important part of international trade.
    a. Export
    b. AD-IA Model
    c. ACCRA Cost of Living Index
    d. ACEA agreement

22. In economics, an _____ is any good (e.g. a commodity) or service brought into one country from another country in a legitimate fashion, typically for use in trade. It is a good that is brought in from another country for sale. _____ goods or services are provided to domestic consumers by foreign producers. An _____ in the receiving country is an export to the sending country.
    a. Import quota
    b. Incoterms
    c. Economic integration
    d. Import

23. The _____ or gross domestic income (GDI), a basic measure of an economy's economic performance, is the market value of all final goods and services produced within the borders of a nation in a year. _____ can be defined in three ways, all of which are conceptually identical. First, it is equal to the total expenditures for all final goods and services produced within the country in a stipulated period of time (usually a 365-day year.)
    a. Countercyclical
    b. Monopolistic competition
    c. Gross domestic product
    d. Market structure

Chapter 3. Demand and Supply

1. In economics, _____ is the total demand for final goods and services in the economy (Y) at a given time and price level. It is the amount of goods and services in the economy that will be purchased at all possible price levels. This is the demand for the gross domestic product of a country when inventory levels are static.
   - a. Aggregation problem
   - b. Aggregate Demand
   - c. Aggregate supply
   - d. Aggregate expenditure

2. Economics:

   - _____,the desire to own something and the ability to pay for it
   - _____ curve,a graphic representation of a _____ schedule
   - _____ deposit, the money in checking accounts
   - _____ pull theory,the theory that inflation occurs when _____ for goods and services exceeds existing supplies
   - _____ schedule,a table that lists the quantity of a good a person will buy it each different price
   - _____ side economics,the school of economics at believes government spending and tax cuts open economy by raising _____

   - a. Production
   - b. Demand
   - c. McKesson ' Robbins scandal
   - d. Variability

3. In economics, a _____ is a table that lists the quantity of a good a person will buy it each different price See Demand curve.
   - a. Free contract
   - b. Demand schedule
   - c. Rational irrationality
   - d. Federal Reserve districts

4. In economics, the _____ is an economic law that states that consumers buy more of a good when its price decreases and less when its price increases.

   There are certain goods which do not follow this law. These include Veblen and Giffen goods

   - a. Law of demand
   - b. Georgism
   - c. Financial crisis
   - d. Market failure

5. CÄ"terÄ«s paribus is a Latin phrase, literally translated as 'with other things the same.' It is commonly rendered in English as 'all other things being equal.' A prediction, or a statement about causal or logical connections between two states of affairs, is qualified by _____ in order to acknowledge, and to rule out, the possibility of other factors which could override the relationship between the antecedent and the consequent.

   A _____ assumption is often fundamental to the predictive purpose of scientific inquiry. In order to formulate scientific laws, it is usually necessary to rule out factors which interfere with examining a specific causal relationship.

   - a. Friedman-Savage utility function
   - b. Capital outflow
   - c. Dematerialization
   - d. Ceteris paribus

Chapter 3. Demand and Supply

6. In economics, the _____ can be defined as the graph depicting the relationship between the price of a certain commodity, and the amount of it that consumers are willing and able to purchase at that given price. It is a graphic representation of a demand schedule. The _____ for all consumers together follows from the _____ of every individual consumer: the individual demands at each price are added together.
   a. Demand curve
   b. Cost curve
   c. Wage curve
   d. Kuznets curve

7. In consumer theory, an _____ is a good that decreases in demand when consumer income rises, unlike normal goods, for which the opposite is observed. It is a good that consumers demand increases when their income increases. Inferiority, in this sense, is an observable fact relating to affordability rather than a statement about the quality of the good.
   a. Export-oriented
   b. Independent goods
   c. Information good
   d. Inferior good

8. In economics, _____s are any goods for which demand increases when income increases and falls when income decreases but price remains constant, i.e. with a positive income elasticity of demand. The term does not necessarily refer to the quality of the good.

Depending on the indifference curves, the amount of a good bought can either increase, decrease, or stay the same when income increases.

   a. Normative economics
   b. Bord halfpenny
   c. Financial contagion
   d. Normal good

9. A _____ is an object whose consumption increases the utility of the consumer, for which the quantity demanded exceeds the quantity supplied at zero price. _____s are usually modeled as having diminishing marginal utility. The first individual purchase has high utility; the second has less.
   a. Pie method
   b. Merit good
   c. Composite good
   d. Good

10. In economics, _____ is the total supply of goods and services produced by a national economy during a specific time period. It is the total amount of goods and services in the economy available at all possible price levels.
    a. Aggregation problem
    b. Aggregate expenditure
    c. Aggregate demand
    d. Aggregate Supply

11. In economics, the _____ is the tendency of suppliers to offer more of a good at a higher price. The relationship between price and quantity supplied is usually a positive relationship. A rise in price is associated with a rise in quantity supplied.
    a. Market failure
    b. Mathematical economics
    c. Heterodox economics
    d. Law of supply

12. In economics, economic equilibrium is simply a state of the world where economic forces are balanced and in the absence of external influences the (equilibrium) values of economic variables will not change. It is the point at which quantity demanded and quantity supplied are equal. _____, for example, refers to a condition where a market price is established through competition such that the amount of goods or services sought by buyers is equal to the amount of goods or services produced by sellers.

Chapter 3. Demand and Supply

a. Regulated market
b. Product-Market Growth Matrix
c. Marketization
d. Market equilibrium

13. _____ in economics and business is the result of an exchange and from that trade we assign a numerical monetary value to a good, service or asset. If Alice trades Bob 4 apples for an orange, the _____ of an orange is 4 apples. Inversely, the _____ of an apple is 1/4 oranges.
   a. Price
   b. Price book
   c. Premium pricing
   d. Price war

14. A _____ is a bond which is worth a certain monetary value and which may only be spent for specific reasons or on specific goods. Examples include -- but are not limited to -- housing, travel and food _____s. The term _____ is also a synonym for receipt, and is often used to refer to receipts used as evidence of, for example, the declaration that a service has been performed or that an expenditure has been made.
   a. 1921 recession
   b. 130-30 fund
   c. 100-year flood
   d. Voucher

15. _____ was an American economist, statistician and public intellectual, and a recipient of the Nobel Memorial Prize in Economic Sciences. He is best known among scholars for his theoretical and empirical research, especially consumption analysis, monetary history and theory, and for his demonstration of the complexity of stabilization policy. A global public followed his restatement of a political philosophy that insisted on minimizing the role of government in favor of the private sector.
   a. Adolph Fischer
   b. Adam Smith
   c. Milton Friedman
   d. Adolf Hitler

Chapter 4. The Power of Prices

1. _____ is a broad label that refers to any individuals or households that use goods and services generated within the economy. The concept of a _____ is used in different contexts, so that the usage and significance of the term may vary.

   Typically when business people and economists talk of _____s they are talking about person as _____, an aggregated commodity item with little individuality other than that expressed in the buy/not-buy decision.

   a. 130-30 fund
   b. 100-year flood
   c. 1921 recession
   d. Consumer

2. The term surplus is used in economics for several related quantities. The _____ is the amount that consumers benefit by being able to purchase a product for a price that is less than they would be willing to pay. The producer surplus is the amount that producers benefit by selling at a market price mechanism that is higher than they would be willing to sell for.
   a. Consumer surplus
   b. Microeconomic reform
   c. Necessity good
   d. Marginal rate of technical substitution

3. _____ in economics and business is the result of an exchange and from that trade we assign a numerical monetary value to a good, service or asset. If Alice trades Bob 4 apples for an orange, the _____ of an orange is 4 apples. Inversely, the _____ of an apple is 1/4 oranges.
   a. Price book
   b. Price war
   c. Premium pricing
   d. Price

4. A _____ is message sent to consumers and producers in the form of a price charged for a commodity; this is seen as indicating a signal for producers to increase supplies and/or consumers to reduce demand.

   For example, in a free price system, rising prices may indicate a shortage of supply, increase in demand, or a rise in input costs. Regardless of the underlying reason--and without the consumer needing to know the cause--the price increase communicates the notion that consumer demand (at this new, higher price) should recede or that supplies should increase.

   a. Mohring effect
   b. Price signal
   c. Market demand schedule
   d. Threshold population

5. In economics and finance, _____ is the change in total cost that arises when the quantity produced changes by one unit. It is the cost of producing one more unit of a good. Mathematically, the _____ function is expressed as the first derivative of the total cost (TC) function with respect to quantity (Q.)
   a. Khozraschyot
   b. Marginal cost
   c. Variable cost
   d. Quality costs

6. The term surplus is used in economics for several related quantities. The consumer surplus is the amount that consumers benefit by being able to purchase a product for a price that is less than they would be willing to pay. The _____ is the amount that producers benefit by selling at a market price mechanism that is higher than they would be willing to sell for.
   a. Schedule delay
   b. Returns to scale
   c. Long term
   d. Producer surplus

Chapter 4. The Power of Prices   17

7. Combined, the consumer surplus, the producer surplus, and the government surplus (if present) make up the _____ or the total surplus. Total surplus is the primary measure used in welfare economics to evaluate the efficiency of a proposed policy.

A basic technique of bargaining for both parties is to pretend that their surplus is less than it really is: sellers may argue that the price they ask hardly leaves them any profit, while customers may play down how eager they are to have the article.

a. National Competition Policy
b. Necessity good
c. Feasibility condition
d. Social surplus

8. A _____ is the space, actual or metaphorical, in which a market operates. The term is also used in a trademark law context to denote the actual consumer environment, ie. the 'real world' in which products and services are provided and consumed.

a. 1921 recession
b. 130-30 fund
c. 100-year flood
d. Marketplace

9. In economics, a _____ is a loss of economic efficiency that can occur when equilibrium for a good or service is not Pareto optimal. In other words, either people who would have more marginal benefit than marginal cost are not buying the good or service, or people who would have more marginal cost than marginal benefit are buying the product.

Causes of _____ can include monopoly pricing, externalities, taxes or subsidies, and binding price ceilings or floors.

a. Leapfrogging
b. Distributive efficiency
c. Contract curve
d. Deadweight loss

10. Many _____ are related to the environmental consequences of production and use

- Systemic risk describes the risks to the overall economy arising from the risks which the banking system takes. That the private costs of banking failure may be smaller than the social costs justifies banking regulations, although regulations could create a moral hazard.

- Anthropogenic climate change is attributed to greenhouse gas emissions from burning oil, gas, and coal. Global warming has been ranked as the #1 externality of all economic activity, in the magnitude of potential harms and yet remains unmitigated.

a. Green certificate
b. Total Economic Value
c. White certificates
d. Negative externalities

11. In economics, a _____ exists when the production or use of goods and services by the market is not efficient. That is, there exists another outcome where all involved can be made better off. _____s can be viewed as scenarios where individuals' pursuit of pure self-interest leads to results that are not efficient - that can be improved upon from the societal point-of-view.

a. Fixed exchange rate
b. Market failure
c. General equilibrium
d. Financial economics

12. In economics, a _____ is a good that is non-rivaled and non-excludable. This means, respectively, that consumption of the good by one individual does not reduce availability of the good for consumption by others; and that no one can be effectively excluded from using the good. In the real world, there may be no such thing as an absolutely non-rivaled and non-excludable good; but economists think that some goods approximate the concept closely enough for the analysis to be economically useful.

a. Public good
b. Happiness economics
c. Demand-pull theory
d. Neoclassical synthesis

Chapter 4. The Power of Prices 19

13. A _____ is:

- Rewrite _____, in generative grammar and computer science
- Standardization, a formal and widely-accepted statement, fact, definition, or qualification
- Operation, a determinate _____ for performing a mathematical operation and obtaining a certain result (Mathematics, Logic)
    - Unary operation
    - Binary operation
- _____ of inference, a function from sets of formulae to formulae (Mathematics, Logic)
- _____ of thumb, principle with broad application that is not intended to be strictly accurate or reliable for every situation. Also often simply referred to as a _____
- Moral, an atomic element of a moral code for guiding choices in human behavior
- Heuristic, a quantized '_____' which shows a tendency or probability for successful function
- A regulation, as in sports
- A Production _____, as in computer science
- Procedural law, a _____ set governing the application of laws to cases
    - A law, which may informally be called a '_____'
    - A court ruling, a decision by a court
- In the U.S. Government, a regulation mandated by Congress, but written or expanded upon by the Executive Branch.
- Norm (sociology), an informal but widely accepted _____, concept, truth, definition, or qualification (social norms, legal norms, coding norms)
- Norm (philosophy), a kind of sentence or a reason to act, feel or believe
- 'Rulership' is the concept of governance by a government:
    - Military _____, governance by a military body
    - Monastic _____, a collection of precepts that guides the life of monks or nuns in a religious order where the superior holds the place of Christ
- Slide _____

- '_____,' a song by Ayumi Hamasaki
- '_____,' a song by rapper Nas
- '_____s,' an album by the band The Whitest Boy Alive
- _____s: Pyaar Ka Superhit Formula, a 2003 Bollywood film
- ruler, an instrument for measuring lengths
- _____, a component of an astrolabe, circumferator or similar instrument
- The _____s, a bestselling self-help book
- _____ Project (Run Up-to-date Linux Everywhere), a project that aims to use up-to-date Linux software on old PCs
- _____ engine, a software system that helps managing business _____s
- Ja _____, a hip hop artist
    - R.U.L.E., a 2005 greatest hits album by rapper Ja _____
- '_____s,' a KMFDM song

a. Rule
b. Technocracy
c. Demand
d. Procter ' Gamble

Chapter 4. The Power of Prices

14. A _____ is an object whose consumption increases the utility of the consumer, for which the quantity demanded exceeds the quantity supplied at zero price. _____s are usually modeled as having diminishing marginal utility. The first individual purchase has high utility; the second has less.
   a. Pie method
   b. Composite good
   c. Merit good
   d. Good

15. In economics, an _____ is any good or commodity, transported from one country to another country in a legitimate fashion, typically for use in trade. _____ goods or services are provided to foreign consumers by domestic producers. _____ is an important part of international trade.
   a. Export
   b. ACCRA Cost of Living Index
   c. ACEA agreement
   d. AD-IA Model

16. In economics, an _____ is any good (e.g. a commodity) or service brought into one country from another country in a legitimate fashion, typically for use in trade. It is a good that is brought in from another country for sale. _____ goods or services are provided to domestic consumers by foreign producers. An _____ in the receiving country is an export to the sending country.
   a. Economic integration
   b. Incoterms
   c. Import
   d. Import quota

17. A _____ is a government imposed limit on how high a price can be charged on a product. For a _____ to be effective, it must differ from the free market price. In the graph at right, the supply and demand curves intersect to determine the free-market quantity and price.
   a. Fire sale
   b. Price ceiling
   c. Pricing
   d. Product sabotage

18. Economic _____ is defined as an excess distribution to any factor in a production process above that which is required to induce the factor into the process or any excess above that which is necessary to keep the factor in its current use..

Classical Factor _____ is primarily concerned with the fee paid for the use of fixed (e.g. natural) resources. The classical definition is expressed as any excess payment above that required to induce or provide for production.

   a. 130-30 fund
   b. 100-year flood
   c. 1921 recession
   d. Rent

19. _____ refers to laws or ordinances that set price controls on the renting of residential housing. It functions as a price ceiling.

_____ exists in approximately 40 countries around the world.

   a. National Housing Conference
   b. Tenant rights
   c. 100-year flood
   d. Rent control

Chapter 4. The Power of Prices

20. In economics, a _____ is a redistribution of income in the market system. These payments are considered to be nonexhaustive because they do not directly absorb resources or create output. Examples of certain _____s include welfare (financial aid), social security, and government subsidies for certain businesses (firms.)
    a. Transfer payment
    b. 130-30 fund
    c. 1921 recession
    d. 100-year flood

21. A _____ is the transfer of wealth from one party (such as a person or company) to another. A _____ is usually made in exchange for the provision of goods, services or both, or to fulfill a legal obligation.

    The simplest and oldest form of _____ is barter, the exchange of one good or service for another.

    a. Payment
    b. Going concern
    c. Soft count
    d. Social gravity

22. A _____ is a bond which is worth a certain monetary value and which may only be spent for specific reasons or on specific goods. Examples include -- but are not limited to -- housing, travel and food _____s. The term _____ is also a synonym for receipt, and is often used to refer to receipts used as evidence of, for example, the declaration that a service has been performed or that an expenditure has been made.
    a. Voucher
    b. 130-30 fund
    c. 100-year flood
    d. 1921 recession

23. A _____ is a government- or group-imposed limit on how low a price can be charged for a product. In order for a _____ to be effective, it must be greater than the equilibrium price. An ineffective _____, below equilibrium price.

    A _____ can be set below the free-market equilibrium price.

    a. Price markdown
    b. Two-part tariff
    c. Flat rate
    d. Price floor

24. In economics, a _____ may be either a subsidy or a price control, both with the intended effect of keeping the market price of a good higher than the competitive equilibrium level.

    In the case of a price control, a _____ is the minimum legal price a seller may charge, typically placed above equilibrium. It is the support of certain price levels at or above market values by the government.

    a. Labor intensity
    b. Payment schedule
    c. Marginal profit
    d. Price support

25. A _____ is the lowest hourly, daily or monthly wage that employers may legally pay to employees or workers. Equivalently, it is the lowest wage at which workers may sell their labor. Although _____ laws are in effect in a great many jurisdictions, there are differences of opinion about the benefits and drawbacks of a _____.
    a. Minimum wage
    b. Microfoundations
    c. Permanent war economy
    d. Marginal propensity to consume

26. The underground economy or _____ is a market where all commerce is conducted without regard to taxation, law or regulations of trade. The term is also often known as the underdog, shadow economy, black economy, parallel economy or phantom trades.

In modern societies the underground economy covers a vast array of activities.

a. Black market
b. Protectionism
c. Social market economy
d. Market economy

27. _____ is the removal or simplification of government rules and regulations that constrain the operation of market forces. _____ does not mean elimination of laws against fraud, but eliminating or reducing government control of how business is done, thereby moving toward a more free market.

The stated rationale for '_____' is often that fewer and simpler regulations will lead to a raised level of competitiveness, therefore higher productivity, more efficiency and lower prices overall.

a. Fundamental psychological law
b. Secular basis
c. Macroeconomic policy instruments
d. Deregulation

Chapter 5. Measuring National Output

1. In macroeconomics, _____ is a condition of the national economy, where all or nearly all persons willing and able to work at the prevailing wages and working conditions are able to do so. It is defined either as 0% unemployment, literally, no unemployment (the rate of unemployment is the fraction of the work force unable to find work), as by James Tobin, or as the level of employment rates when there is no cyclical unemployment. It is defined by the majority of mainstream economists as being an acceptable level of natural unemployment above 0%, the discrepancy from 0% being due to non-cyclical types of unemployment.
   - a. Harrod-Johnson diagram
   - b. Demand shock
   - c. Full employment
   - d. Marginal propensity to consume

2. _____ is a branch of economics that deals with the performance, structure, and behavior of a national or regional economy as a whole. Along with microeconomics, _____ is one of the two most general fields in economics. It is the study of the behavior and decision-making of entire economies.
   - a. Tobit model
   - b. New Trade Theory
   - c. Macroeconomics
   - d. Nominal value

Chapter 5. Measuring National Output

3. A _____ is:

- Rewrite _____, in generative grammar and computer science
- Standardization, a formal and widely-accepted statement, fact, definition, or qualification
- Operation, a determinate _____ for performing a mathematical operation and obtaining a certain result (Mathematics, Logic)
    - Unary operation
    - Binary operation
- _____ of inference, a function from sets of formulae to formulae (Mathematics, Logic)
- _____ of thumb, principle with broad application that is not intended to be strictly accurate or reliable for every situation. Also often simply referred to as a _____
- Moral, an atomic element of a moral code for guiding choices in human behavior
- Heuristic, a quantized '_____' which shows a tendency or probability for successful function
- A regulation, as in sports
- A Production _____, as in computer science
- Procedural law, a _____ set governing the application of laws to cases
    - A law, which may informally be called a '_____'
    - A court ruling, a decision by a court
- In the U.S. Government, a regulation mandated by Congress, but written or expanded upon by the Executive Branch.
- Norm (sociology), an informal but widely accepted _____, concept, truth, definition, or qualification (social norms, legal norms, coding norms)
- Norm (philosophy), a kind of sentence or a reason to act, feel or believe
- 'Rulership' is the concept of governance by a government:
    - Military _____, governance by a military body
    - Monastic _____, a collection of precepts that guides the life of monks or nuns in a religious order where the superior holds the place of Christ
- Slide _____

- '_____,' a song by Ayumi Hamasaki
- '_____,' a song by rapper Nas
- '_____s,' an album by the band The Whitest Boy Alive
- _____s: Pyaar Ka Superhit Formula, a 2003 Bollywood film
- ruler, an instrument for measuring lengths
- _____, a component of an astrolabe, circumferator or similar instrument
- The _____s, a bestselling self-help book
- _____ Project (Run Up-to-date Linux Everywhere), a project that aims to use up-to-date Linux software on old PCs
- _____ engine, a software system that helps managing business _____s
- Ja _____, a hip hop artist
    - R.U.L.E., a 2005 greatest hits album by rapper Ja _____
- '_____s,' a KMFDM song

a. Demand　　　　　　　　　　　　b. Procter ' Gamble
c. Technocracy　　　　　　　　　　d. Rule

Chapter 5. Measuring National Output

4. _____s is the social science that studies the production, distribution, and consumption of goods and services. The term _____s comes from the Ancient Greek oá¼°κονομῖα from oá¼¶κος (oikos, 'house') + vΐŒμος (nomos, 'custom' or 'law'), hence 'rules of the house(hold)'. Current _____ models developed out of the broader field of political economy in the late 19th century, owing to a desire to use an empirical approach more akin to the physical sciences.
   a. Energy economics
   b. Opportunity cost
   c. Inflation
   d. Economic

5. The _____ or gross domestic income (GDI), a basic measure of an economy's economic performance, is the market value of all final goods and services produced within the borders of a nation in a year. _____ can be defined in three ways, all of which are conceptually identical. First, it is equal to the total expenditures for all final goods and services produced within the country in a stipulated period of time (usually a 365-day year.)
   a. Countercyclical
   b. Monopolistic competition
   c. Market structure
   d. Gross domestic product

6. _____ is generally measured by standards such as real (i.e. inflation adjusted) income per person and poverty rate. Other measures such as access and quality of health care, income growth inequality and educational standards are also used. Examples are access to certain goods (such as number of refrigerators per 1000 people), or measures of health such as life expectancy.
   a. 130-30 fund
   b. 100-year flood
   c. Standard of living
   d. Remuneration

7. _____ is a common concept in economics, and gives rise to derived concepts such as consumer debt. Generally _____ is defined by opposition to production. But the precise definition can vary because different schools of economists define production quite differently.
   a. Federal Reserve Bank Notes
   b. Consumption
   c. Foreclosure data providers
   d. Cash or share options

8. In economics _____s are goods that are ultimately consumed rather than used in the production of another good. For example, a car sold to a consumer is a _____; the components such as tires sold to the car manufacturer are not; they are intermediate goods used to make the _____.

   When used in measures of national income and output the term _____s only includes new goods.

   a. Substitute good
   b. Luxury good
   c. Goods and services
   d. Final good

9. _____ or producer goods are goods used as inputs in the production of other goods, such as partly finished goods. They are goods used in production of final goods. A firm may make then use _____, or make then sell, or buy then use them.
   a. Income distribution
   b. Inflation adjustment
   c. Economic forecasting
   d. Intermediate goods

10. _____ is the price at which an asset would trade in a competitive Walrasian auction setting. _____ is often used interchangeably with open _____, fair value or fair _____, although these terms have distinct definitions in different standards, and may differ in some circumstances.

International Valuation Standards defines _____ as 'the estimated amount for which a property should exchange on the date of valuation between a willing buyer and a willing seller in an arm's-length transaction after proper marketing wherein the parties had each acted knowledgeably, prudently, and without compulsion.'

_____ is a concept distinct from market price, which is 'the price at which one can transact', while _____ is 'the true underlying value' according to theoretical standards.

a. Personal financial management
b. Secured loan
c. Netting
d. Market value

11. A _____ is an object whose consumption increases the utility of the consumer, for which the quantity demanded exceeds the quantity supplied at zero price. _____s are usually modeled as having diminishing marginal utility. The first individual purchase has high utility; the second has less.

a. Pie method
b. Merit good
c. Composite good
d. Good

12. _____ is the a method of technical and economic research of the systems for purpose to optimize a parity between system's consumer functions or properties and expenses to achieve those functions or properties.

This methodology for continuous perfection of production, industrial technologies, organizational structures was developed by Juryj Sobolev in 1948 at the 'Perm telephone factory'

- 1948 Juryj Sobolev - the first success in application of a method analysis at the 'Perm telephone factory' .
- 1949 - the first application for the invention as result of use of the new method.

Today in economically developed countries practically each enterprise or the company use methodology of the kind of functional-cost analysis as a practice of the quality management, most full satisfying to principles of standards of series ISO 9000.

- Interest of consumer not in products itself, but the advantage which it will receive from its usage.
- The consumer aspires to reduce his expenses
- Functions needed by consumer can be executed in the various ways, and, hence, with various efficiency and expenses. Among possible alternatives of realization of functions exist such in which the parity of quality and the price is the optimal for the consumer.

The goal of _____ is achievement of the highest consumer satisfaction of production at simultaneous decrease in all kinds of industrial expenses Classical _____ has three English synonyms - Value Engineering, Value Management, Value Analysis.

a. Willingness to pay
b. Staple financing
c. Monopoly wage
d. Function cost analysis

13. _____ is the measure of investment used to compute GDP. This is an important component of GDP because it provides an indicator of the future productive capacity of the economy. It includes replacement purchases plus net additions to capital assets plus investments in inventories.
   a. Compensation of employees
   b. Gross private domestic investment
   c. Current account
   d. National Income and Product Accounts

14. The _____ equals the gross domestic product (GDP) minus depreciation on a country's capital goods.

   _____ accounts for capital that has been consumed over the year in the form of housing, vehicle, or machinery deterioration. The depreciation accounted for is often referred to as capital consumption allowance and represents the amount needed in order to replace those depreciated assets.

   a. Carrying charge
   b. Cass criterion
   c. Net domestic product
   d. Commodity price shocks

15. In economics, _____ refers to an activity of spending which increases the availability of fixed capital goods or means of production. It is the total spending on new fixed investment minus replacement investment, which simply replaces depreciated capital goods.
   a. Greenfield investment
   b. Lehman Formula
   c. Tangible investments
   d. Net investment

16. _____ in economics and business is the result of an exchange and from that trade we assign a numerical monetary value to a good, service or asset. If Alice trades Bob 4 apples for an orange, the _____ of an orange is 4 apples. Inversely, the _____ of an apple is 1/4 oranges.
   a. Price war
   b. Premium pricing
   c. Price book
   d. Price

17. A _____ is a normalized average (typically a weighted average) of prices for a given class of goods or services in a given region, during a given interval of time. It is a statistic designed to help to compare how these prices, taken as a whole, differ between time periods or geographical locations.

   Price indices have several potential uses.

   a. Transactional Net Margin Method
   b. Product sabotage
   c. Two-part tariff
   d. Price index

18. _____ refers to a business or organization attempting to acquire goods or services to accomplish the goals of the enterprise. Though there are several organizations that attempt to set standards in the _____ process, processes can vary greatly between organizations. Typically the word '_____' is not used interchangeably with the word 'procurement', since procurement typically includes Expediting, Supplier Quality, and Traffic and Logistics (T'L) in addition to _____.
   a. 130-30 fund
   b. Free port
   c. Purchasing
   d. 100-year flood

19. In economics, a _____ is a redistribution of income in the market system. These payments are considered to be nonexhaustive because they do not directly absorb resources or create output. Examples of certain _____s include welfare (financial aid), social security, and government subsidies for certain businesses (firms).

a. 100-year flood
c. Transfer payment
b. 1921 recession
d. 130-30 fund

20. In economics, an _____ is any good or commodity, transported from one country to another country in a legitimate fashion, typically for use in trade. _____ goods or services are provided to foreign consumers by domestic producers. _____ is an important part of international trade.
   a. ACEA agreement
   c. ACCRA Cost of Living Index
   b. AD-IA Model
   d. Export

21. A _____ is the transfer of wealth from one party (such as a person or company) to another. A _____ is usually made in exchange for the provision of goods, services or both, or to fulfill a legal obligation.

The simplest and oldest form of _____ is barter, the exchange of one good or service for another.

   a. Social gravity
   c. Soft count
   b. Going concern
   d. Payment

22. In economics, the term _____ of income or _____ refers to a simple economic model which describes the reciprocal circulation of income between producers and consumers. In the _____ model, the inter-dependent entities of producer and consumer are referred to as 'firms' and 'households' respectively and provide each other with factors in order to facilitate the flow of income. Firms provide consumers with goods and services in exchange for consumer expenditure and 'factors of production' from households.
   a. 1921 recession
   c. 100-year flood
   b. 130-30 fund
   d. Circular flow

23. The cost advantages of using _____ include:

   - Reconciling conflicting preferences of lenders and borrowers

   - Risk aversion- intermediaries help spread out and decrease the risks

   - Economies of scale- using _____ reduces the costs of lending and borrowing

   - Economies of scope- intermediaries concentrate on the demands of the lenders and borrowers and are able to enhance their products and services (use same inputs to produce different outputs)

_____ include:

   - Banks
   - Building societies
   - Credit unions
   - Financial advisers or brokers
   - Insurance companies
   - Collective investment schemes
   - Pension funds

Chapter 5. Measuring National Output

Financial institutions (intermediaries) perform the vital role of bringing together those economic agents with surplus funds who want to lend, with those with a shortage of funds who want to borrow.

In doing this they offer the major benefits of maturity and risk transformation. It is possible for this to be done by direct contact between the ultimate borrowers, but there are major cost disadvantages of direct finance.

Indeed, one explanation of the existence of specialist _____ is that they have a related (cost) advantage in offering financial services, which not only enables them to make profit, but also raises the overall efficiency of the economy.

- a. Financial intermediaries
- b. Broker-dealer
- c. SICAV
- d. Collective investment scheme

24. In economics, a _____ is a mechanism that allows people to easily buy and sell (trade) financial securities (such as stocks and bonds), commodities (such as precious metals or agricultural goods), and other fungible items of value at low transaction costs and at prices that reflect the efficient-market hypothesis.

_____s have evolved significantly over several hundred years and are undergoing constant innovation to improve liquidity.

Both general markets (where many commodities are traded) and specialized markets (where only one commodity is traded) exist.

- a. Convertible arbitrage
- b. Market anomaly
- c. Noise trader
- d. Financial market

25. The _____ consists of a number of economic theories which describe the nature of the firm, company including its existence, its behaviour, and its relationship with the market.

In simplified terms, the _____ aims to answer these questions:

1. Existence - why do firms emerge, why are not all transactions in the economy mediated over the market?
2. Boundaries - why the boundary between firms and the market is located exactly there? Which transactions are performed internally and which are negotiated on the market?
3. Organization - why are firms structured in such specific way? What is the interplay of formal and informal relationships?

Despite looking simple, these questions are not answered by the established economic theory, which usually views firms as given, and treats them as black boxes without any internal structure.

The First World War period saw a change of emphasis in economic theory away from industry-level analysis which mainly included analysing markets to analysis at the level of the firm, as it became increasingly clear that perfect competition was no longer an adequate model of how firms behaved. Economic theory till then had focussed on trying to understand markets alone and there had been little study on understanding why firms or organisations exist.

    a. Policy Ineffectiveness Proposition   b. Khazzoom-Brookes postulate
    c. Technology gap   d. Theory of the firm

26. The _____ is one of three major groups of methodologies, called valuation approaches, used by appraisers. It is particularly common in commercial real estate appraisal and in business appraisal. The fundamental math is similar to the methods used for financial valuation, securities analysis, or bond pricing.
    a. ACCRA Cost of Living Index   b. Urban growth boundary
    c. Income approach   d. ACEA agreement

27. _____ is a fee paid on borrowed assets. It is the price paid for the use of borrowed money , or, money earned by deposited funds . Assets that are sometimes lent with _____ include money, shares, consumer goods through hire purchase, major assets such as aircraft, and even entire factories in finance lease arrangements.
    a. Internal debt   b. Interest
    c. Asset protection   d. Insolvency

28. The _____ is the percentage of the Gross Domestic Product (GDP) which is due to depreciation. The _____ measures the amount of expenditure that a country needs to undertake in order to maintain, as opposed to grow, its productivity. The _____ can be thought of as representing the wear-and-tear on the country's physical capital, together with the investment needed to maintain the level of human capital (eg to educate the workers needed to replace retirees.)
    a. Gross domestic product per barrel   b. Skyscraper Index
    c. Water footprint   d. Capital consumption allowance

29. _____ is a term used in accounting, economics and finance to spread the cost of an asset over the span of several years.

In simple words we can say that _____ is the reduction in the value of an asset due to usage, passage of time, wear and tear, technological outdating or obsolescence, depletion, inadequacy, rot, rust, decay or other such factors.

In accounting, _____ is a term used to describe any method of attributing the historical or purchase cost of an asset across its useful life, roughly corresponding to normal wear and tear.

    a. Salvage value   b. Depreciation
    c. Net income per employee   d. Historical cost

30. _____ is equal to the income that a firm has after subtracting costs and expenses from the total revenue. _____ can be distributed among holders of common stock as a dividend or held by the firm as retained earnings. _____ is an accounting term.

Chapter 5. Measuring National Output

a. Historical cost
b. Net profit
c. Salvage value
d. Net income

31. To _____ is to impose a financial charge or other levy upon a taxpayer by a state or the functional equivalent of a state.

_____es are also imposed by many subnational entities. _____es consist of direct _____ or indirect _____, and may be paid in money or as its labour equivalent (often but not always unpaid.)

a. 1921 recession
b. Tax
c. 100-year flood
d. 130-30 fund

32. To tax is to impose a financial charge or other levy upon a taxpayer by a state or the functional equivalent of a state.

_____ are also imposed by many subnational entities. _____ consist of direct tax or indirect tax, and may be paid in money or as its labour equivalent (often but not always unpaid.)

a. 130-30 fund
b. 1921 recession
c. 100-year flood
d. Taxes

33. _____ is a misspelled phrase from Latin 'pro capite' phrase meaning per head with pro meaning 'per' or 'for each' and capite meaning 'head.' Both words together equate to the phrase 'for each head.'

It is usually used in the field of statistics to indicate the average per person for any given concern, such as income, crime rate, etc.

It is also used in wills to indicate that each of the named beneficiaries should receive, by devise or bequest, equal shares of the estate. This is in contrast to a per stirpes division, in which each branch of the inheriting family inherits an equal share of the estate.

a. False positive rate
b. Sargan test
c. Population statistics
d. Per capita

34. A variety of measures of national income and output are used in economics to estimate total economic activity in a country or region, including gross domestic product (GDP), _____ , and net national income (NNI.)

There are three main ways of calculating these numbers; the output approach, the income approach and the expenditure approach. In theory, the three must yield the same, because total expenditures on goods and services must equal the total income paid to the producers (GNI), and that must also equal the total value of the output of goods and services (_____.)

a. Gross national product
b. Household final consumption expenditure
c. Gross world product
d. Purchasing power parity

Chapter 5. Measuring National Output

35. _____ refers to the additional value of a commodity over the cost of commodities used to produce it from the previous stage of production. An example is the price of gasoline at the pump over the price of the oil in it. In national accounts used in macroeconomics, it refers to the contribution of the factors of production, i.e., land, labor, and capital goods, to raising the value of a product and corresponds to the incomes received by the owners of these factors.
   a. Full employment
   b. Hodrick-Prescott filter
   c. Solow residual
   d. Value added

36. The _____ is 'the basic residential unit in which economic production, consumption, inheritance, child rearing, and shelter are organized and carried out'; [the _____] 'may or may not be synonomous with family'.

The _____ is the basic unit of analysis in many social, microeconomic and government models. The term refers to all individuals who live in the same dwelling.

   a. Family economics
   b. 130-30 fund
   c. 100-year flood
   d. Household

37. The _____ or black market is a market where all commerce is conducted without regard to taxation, law or regulations of trade. The term is also often known as the underdog, shadow economy, black economy, parallel economy or phantom trades.

In modern societies the _____ covers a vast array of activities.

   a. Autarky
   b. Information economy
   c. Information markets
   d. Underground economy

38. In microeconomics, _____ is quite simply the conversion of inputs into outputs. It is an economic process that uses resources to create a good or service that is suitable for exchange. This can include manufacturing, storing, shipping, and packaging.
   a. Red Guards
   b. Solved
   c. MET
   d. Production

39. An _____, in economics, is the amount by which the real Gross domestic product exceeds potential GDP. The real GDP is also known as GDP 'adjusted for inflation', 'constant prices' GDP or 'constant dollar' GDP, because it measures the aggregate output in a country's income accounts in a given year, expressed in base-year prices. On the other hand, the potential GDP is the quantity of real GDP when a country's economy is at full-employment.
   a. AD-IA Model
   b. Inflationary gap
   c. ACCRA Cost of Living Index
   d. ACEA agreement

40. The term _____ refers to economy-wide fluctuations in production or economic activity over several months or years. These fluctuations occur around a long-term growth trend, and typically involve shifts over time between periods of relatively rapid economic growth (expansion or boom), and periods of relative stagnation or decline (contraction or recession.)

These fluctuations are often measured using the growth rate of real gross domestic product.

Chapter 5. Measuring National Output

a. Tobit model
c. Nominal value
b. Business cycle
d. Consumer theory

41. In economics, a _____ is a general slowdown in economic activity over a sustained period of time, or a business cycle contraction. During _____s, many macroeconomic indicators vary in a similar way. Production as measured by Gross Domestic Product (GDP), employment, investment spending, capacity utilization, household incomes and business profits all fall during _____s.
   a. Treasury View
   c. Monetary economics
   b. Leading indicators
   d. Recession

42. In economic models, the _____ time frame assumes no fixed factors of production. Firms can enter or leave the marketplace, and the cost (and availability) of land, labor, raw materials, and capital goods can be assumed to vary. In contrast, in the short-run time frame, certain factors are assumed to be fixed, because there is not sufficient time for them to change.
   a. Diseconomies of scale
   c. Price/performance ratio
   b. Productivity world
   d. Long-run

43. In economics, the concept of the _____ refers to the decision-making time frame of a firm in which at least one factor of production is fixed. Costs which are fixed in the _____ have no impact on a firms decisions. For example a firm can raise output by increasing the amount of labour through overtime.
   a. Hicks-neutral technical change
   c. Product Pipeline
   b. Productivity model
   d. Short-run

44. _____ is a statistical method for removing the seasonal component of a time series used when analyzing non-seasonal trends.

The investigation of many economic time series becomes problematic due to seasonal fluctuations. Series are made up of four components:

S_t: The Seasonal Component

T_t: The Trend Component

C_t: The Cyclical Component

I_t: The Error, or irregular component.

   a. Partial autocorrelation
   c. Granger causality
   b. Seasonality
   d. Seasonal adjustment

45. A _____ is an economic indicator that reacts slowly to economic changes, and therefore has little predictive value. Generally these types of indicators follow an event; they are historical in nature. For example, in a performance measuring system, profit earned by a business is a _____ as it reflects a historical performance; similarly, improved customer satisfaction is the result of initiatives taken in the past.

a. Bureau of Labor Statistics
b. Nonfarm payrolls
c. Skyscraper Index
d. Lagging indicator

46. In economics, _____ are key economic variables that economists used to predict a new phase of the business cycle. A leading indicator is one that changes before the economy does; a lagging indicator is one that changes after the economy has changed. Examples of _____ include stock prices, which often improve or worsen before a similar change in the economy.

a. Gross domestic product
b. Medium of exchange
c. Macroeconomics
d. Leading indicators

47. _____ predicts the impact of fiscal policy changes by forecasting the effects of economic agents' reactions to policy. It is an adaptation of static scoring, the traditional method for analyzing policy changes.

The method yields a more accurate prediction of a policy's impact on a country's fiscal balance and economic output when it can be performed accurately.

a. 100-year flood
b. Sustainable investment rule
c. Dynamic scoring
d. Fiscal policy

48. The term _____ refers to government debt, expenditures and revenues, or to finance (particularly financial revenue) in general.

- _____ deficit is the budget deficit of federal or local government
- _____ policy is the discretionary spending of governments. Contrasts with monetary policy.
- _____ year and _____ quarter are reporting periods for firms and other agencies.

a. Procter ' Gamble
b. Drawdown
c. Bucket shop
d. Fiscal

49. _____ is the term used by governments to describe a monetary imbalance between the national government and smaller, subordinate governments, such as those of states or provinces.

A vertical _____ occurs when the revenues of different levels of government do not match their expenditure responsibilities. This will necessitate transfer payments from the overendowed party to the underendowed party (vertical fiscal equalization.)

a. Lucas critique
b. Fiscal imbalance
c. Peak-load pricing
d. Ramsey problem

50. A variety of measures of _____ and output are used in economics to estimate total economic activity in a country or region, including gross domestic product (GDP), gross national product (GNP), and net _____.

Chapter 5. Measuring National Output 35

There are three main ways of calculating these numbers; the output approach, the income approach and the expenditure approach. In theory, the three must yield the same, because total expenditures on goods and services must equal the total income paid to the producers (Gnational income), and that must also equal the total value of the output of goods and services (GNP.)

- a. GNI per capita
- b. Volume index
- c. Gross world product
- d. National income

51. _____ is the total market value of all final goods and services produced by citizens of an economy during a given period of time (gross national product or GNP) minus depreciation. The _____ can be similarly applied at a country's domestic output level. The net domestic product (NDP) is the equivalent application of _____ within macroeconomics, and NDP is equal to gross domestic product (GDP) minus depreciation: NDP = GDP - depreciation.
- a. Compensation of employees
- b. Gross private domestic investment
- c. Current account
- d. Net national product

52. The _____ is the component statistic for consumption in GDP collected by the BEA. It consists of the actual and imputed expenditures of households and includes data pertaining to durable and non-durable goods, and services. It is essentially a measure of goods and services targeted towards individuals and consumed by individuals.
- a. Hemline index
- b. State Domestic Product
- c. Real gross domestic product
- d. Personal consumption expenditure

53. A _____ product is a product designed for cheapness and short-term convenience rather than medium to long-term durability, with most products only intended for single use. The term is also sometimes used for products that may last several months (ex. _____ air filters) to distinguish from similar products that last indefinitely (ex.
- a. 100-year flood
- b. Disposable
- c. 130-30 fund
- d. 1921 recession

54. Disposable income is gross income minus income tax on that income. In national accounts definitions, personal income, minus personal current taxes equals _____. Subtracting personal outlays (which includes the major category of [[personal [or, private] consumption expenditure]]) yields personal (or, private) savings.
- a. Tax harmonization
- b. Tax resistance
- c. Tax revolt
- d. Disposable personal income

55. Total _____ is defined by the United States' Bureau of Economic Analysis as

income received by persons from all sources. It includes income received from participation in production as well as from government and business transfer payments. It is the sum of compensation of employees (received), supplements to wages and salaries, proprietors' income with inventory valuation adjustment (IVA) and capital consumption adjustment (CCAdj), rental income of persons with CCAdj, _____ receipts on assets, and personal current transfer receipts, less contributions for government social insurance.

- a. Bidding
- b. Greater fool theory
- c. Dividend Discount Model
- d. Personal income

Chapter 5. Measuring National Output

56. _____ use double-entry accounting to report the monetary value and sources of output produced in a country and the distribution of incomes that production generates. Data are available at the national and industry levels.

The NIPA summarizes national income on the left (debit, revenue) side and national product on the right (credit, expense) side of a two-column accounting report.

a. Net national product
b. Gross private domestic investment
c. National income and product accounts
d. Current account

Chapter 6. Unemployment

1. In economics, the people in the _____ are the suppliers of labor. The _____ is all the nonmilitary people who are employed or unemployed. In 2005, the worldwide _____ was over 3 billion people.
    a. Departmentalization
    b. Distributed workforce
    c. Grenelle agreements
    d. Labor force

2. Economists distinguish between various types of unemployment, including _____, frictional unemployment, structural unemployment and classical unemployment. Some additional types of unemployment that are occasionally mentioned are seasonal unemployment, hardcore unemployment, and hidden unemployment. Real-world unemployment may combine different types.
    a. Seasonal unemployment
    b. Cyclical unemployment
    c. Structural unemployment
    d. Types of unemployment

3. Unemployment occurs when a person is available to work and seeking work but currently without work. The prevalence of unemployment is usually measured using the _____, which is defined as the percentage of those in the labor force who are unemployed. The _____ is also used in economic studies and economic indexes such as the United States' Conference Board's Index of Leading Indicators as a measure of the state of the macroeconomics.
    a. AD-IA Model
    b. ACCRA Cost of Living Index
    c. ACEA agreement
    d. Unemployment rate

4. The _____ or gross domestic income (GDI), a basic measure of an economy's economic performance, is the market value of all final goods and services produced within the borders of a nation in a year. _____ can be defined in three ways, all of which are conceptually identical. First, it is equal to the total expenditures for all final goods and services produced within the country in a stipulated period of time (usually a 365-day year.)
    a. Gross domestic product
    b. Market structure
    c. Countercyclical
    d. Monopolistic competition

5. In economics, a _____ is a person of legal employment age who is not actively seeking employment. This is usually due to the fact that an individual has given up looking or has had no success in finding a job, hence the term 'discouraged.' Their belief may derive from a variety of factors including: a shortage of jobs in their locality or line of work; perceived discrimination for reasons such as age, race, sex and religion; a lack of necessary skills, training or experience; or, a chronic illness or disability. Some _____s, however, are voluntarily unemployed such as stay-at-home parents, pregnant mothers, and will beneficiaries.
    a. Relative income hypothesis
    b. Hedonimetry
    c. Demand side economics
    d. Discouraged worker

6. The _____ or black market is a market where all commerce is conducted without regard to taxation, law or regulations of trade. The term is also often known as the underdog, shadow economy, black economy, parallel economy or phantom trades.

    In modern societies the _____ covers a vast array of activities.

    a. Underground economy
    b. Autarky
    c. Information markets
    d. Information economy

7. In finance, the _____ of a financial asset measures the sensitivity of the asset's price to interest rate movements. There are various definitions of _____ and derived quantities, discussed below. If not otherwise specified, '_____' generally means the Macaulay _____, as defined below.

a. Time value of money
b. 100-year flood
c. Newtonian time
d. Duration

8. Economists distinguish between various types of unemployment, including cyclical unemployment, _____, structural unemployment and classical unemployment. Some additional types of unemployment that are occasionally mentioned are seasonal unemployment, hardcore unemployment, and hidden unemployment. Real-world unemployment may combine different types.
   a. Types of unemployment
   b. Structural unemployment
   c. Frictional unemployment
   d. Seasonal unemployment

9. Though there have been several definitions of voluntary and _____ in the economics literature, a simple distinction is often applied. Voluntary unemployment is attributed to the individual's decisions, whereas _____ exists because of the socio-economic environment (including the market structure, government intervention, and the level of aggregate demand) in which individuals operate. In these terms, much or most of frictional unemployment is voluntary, since it reflects individual search behavior.
   a. ACEA agreement
   b. Involuntary unemployment
   c. AD-IA Model
   d. ACCRA Cost of Living Index

10. Economists distinguish between various types of unemployment, including cyclical unemployment, frictional unemployment, structural unemployment and classical unemployment. Some additional types of unemployment that are occasionally mentioned are _____, hardcore unemployment, and hidden unemployment. Real-world unemployment may combine different types.
    a. Graduate unemployment
    b. Structural unemployment
    c. Frictional unemployment
    d. Seasonal unemployment

11. _____ is long-term and chronic unemployment arising from imbalances between the skills and other characteristics of workers in the market and the needs of employers. It involves a mismatch between workers looking for jobs and the vacancies available often despite the number of vacancies being similar to the number of unemployed people. In this case, the unemployed workers lack the specific skills required for the jobs, or are located in a different geographical region to the vacant jobs.
    a. Types of unemployment
    b. Frictional unemployment
    c. Seasonal unemployment
    d. Structural unemployment

12. _____ refers to the stock of skills and knowledge embodied in the ability to perform labor so as to produce economic value. It is the skills and knowledge gained by a worker through education and experience. Many early economic theories refer to it simply as labor, one of three factors of production, and consider it to be a fungible resource -- homogeneous and easily interchangeable. Other conceptions of labor dispense with these assumptions.
    a. Human capital
    b. Price theory
    c. Law of increasing costs
    d. General equilibrium

13. _____, in law and economics, is a form of risk management primarily used to hedge against the risk of a contingent loss. _____ is defined as the equitable transfer of the risk of a loss, from one entity to another, in exchange for a premium, and can be thought of as a guaranteed small loss to prevent a large, possibly devastating loss. An insurer is a company selling the _____; an insured or policyholder is the person or entity buying the _____.

a. AD-IA Model
b. ACCRA Cost of Living Index
c. ACEA agreement
d. Insurance

14. The _____ is a concept of economic activity developed in particular by Milton Friedman and Edmund Phelps in the 1960s, both recipients of the Nobel prize in economics. In both cases, the development of the concept is cited as a main motivation behind the prize. It represents the hypothetical unemployment rate consistent with aggregate production being at the 'long-run' level.
   a. Robertson lag
   b. Romer Model
   c. Real Business Cycle Theory
   d. Natural rate of unemployment

15. Wisconsin originated the idea of _____ in the U.S. in 1932. In the United States, there are 50 state _____ programs plus one each in the District of Columbia and Puerto Rico. Through the Social Security Act of 1935, the Federal Government of the United States effectively coerced the individual states into adopting _____ plans.
   a. ACCRA Cost of Living Index
   b. ACEA agreement
   c. AD-IA Model
   d. Unemployment insurance

16. In macroeconomics, _____ is a condition of the national economy, where all or nearly all persons willing and able to work at the prevailing wages and working conditions are able to do so. It is defined either as 0% unemployment, literally, no unemployment (the rate of unemployment is the fraction of the work force unable to find work), as by James Tobin, or as the level of employment rates when there is no cyclical unemployment. It is defined by the majority of mainstream economists as being an acceptable level of natural unemployment above 0%, the discrepancy from 0% being due to non-cyclical types of unemployment.
   a. Demand shock
   b. Marginal propensity to consume
   c. Harrod-Johnson diagram
   d. Full employment

Chapter 7. Inflation

1. In economics, _____ is a sustained decrease in the general price level of goods and services. _____ occurs when the annual inflation rate falls below zero percent, resulting in an increase in the real value of money -- a negative inflation rate. This should not be confused with disinflation, a slow-down in the inflation rate (i.e. when the inflation decreases, but still remains positive.)

   a. Deflation
   b. Literacy rate
   c. Price revolution
   d. Tobit model

2. The _____ or gross domestic income (GDI), a basic measure of an economy's economic performance, is the market value of all final goods and services produced within the borders of a nation in a year. _____ can be defined in three ways, all of which are conceptually identical. First, it is equal to the total expenditures for all final goods and services produced within the country in a stipulated period of time (usually a 365-day year.)

   a. Countercyclical
   b. Gross domestic product
   c. Monopolistic competition
   d. Market structure

3. _____ in economics and business is the result of an exchange and from that trade we assign a numerical monetary value to a good, service or asset. If Alice trades Bob 4 apples for an orange, the _____ of an orange is 4 apples. Inversely, the _____ of an apple is 1/4 oranges.

   a. Price war
   b. Premium pricing
   c. Price book
   d. Price

4. A _____ is a hypothetical measure of overall prices for some set of goods and services, in a given region during a given interval, normalized relative to some base set. Typically, a _____ is approximated with a price index.

   The classical dichotomy is the assumption that there is a relatively clean distinction between overall increases or decreases in prices and underlying, e;reale; economic variables.

   a. Price level
   b. Discretionary spending
   c. Discouraged worker
   d. Price elasticity of supply

5. In statistics, a _____ is a value that allows data to be measured over time in terms of some base period usually through a price index in order to distinguish between changes in the money value of GNP which result from a change in prices and those which result from a change in physical output. It is the measure of the price level for some quantity. A _____ serves as a price index in which the effects of inflation are nulled.

   a. Blanket order
   b. Deflator
   c. Contingent employment
   d. Market microstructure

6. In economics, _____ is a rise in the general level of prices of goods and services in an economy over a period of time. When the general price level rises, each unit of currency buys fewer goods and services; consequently, _____ is also a decline in the real value of money--a loss of purchasing power in the medium of exchange which is also the monetary unit of account in the economy. A chief measure of general price-level _____ is the general _____ rate, which is the percentage change in a general price index (normally the Consumer Price Index) over time.

   a. Energy economics
   b. Opportunity cost
   c. Economic
   d. Inflation

7. In economics, the _____ is a measure of inflation, the rate of increase of a price index (for example, a consumer price index.)It is the percentage rate of change in price level over time. The rate of decrease in the purchasing power of money is approximately equal.

Chapter 7. Inflation

It's used to calculate the real interest rate, as well as real increases in wages, and official measurements of this rate act as input variables to COLA adjustments and Inflation derivatives prices.

- a. Interest rate option
- b. Inflation rate
- c. Equity value
- d. Edgeworth paradox

8. In economics, an _____ is any good or commodity, transported from one country to another country in a legitimate fashion, typically for use in trade. _____ goods or services are provided to foreign consumers by domestic producers. _____ is an important part of international trade.
   - a. ACCRA Cost of Living Index
   - b. AD-IA Model
   - c. ACEA agreement
   - d. Export

9. _____ is a decrease in the rate of inflation. This phase of the business cycle, in which retailers can no longer pass on higher prices to their customers, often occurs during a recession. In contrast, deflation occurs when prices are actually dropping.
   - a. Mundell-Tobin effect
   - b. Reflation
   - c. Disinflation
   - d. Stealth inflation

10. _____ occurs when the inhabitants of a country use foreign currency in parallel to or instead of the domestic currency.

    _____ can occur

    - unofficially, when private agents prefer the foreign currency over the domestic currency. They hold for example deposits in the foreign currency because of a bad track record of the local currency.
    - semiofficially (or officially bimonetary systems), where foreign currency is legal tender, but plays a secondary role to domestic currency
    - officially, when a country ceases to issue the domestic currency and uses only foreign currency. It adopts the foreign currency as legal tender.

    The term _____ is not only applied to usage of the United States dollar, but also generally to the use of any foreign currency as the national currency.

    - a. Commodity money
    - b. World currency
    - c. Currency board
    - d. Dollarization

11. _____ is the rate of inflation excluding the effects of food and energy prices.
    - a. Headline inflation
    - b. Cost-push inflation
    - c. Symmetrical inflation target
    - d. Core inflation

12. _____ is the cost of maintaining a certain standard of living. Changes in the _____ over time are often operationalized in a _____ index. _____ calculations are also used to compare the cost of maintaining a certain standard of living in different geographic areas.

42   *Chapter 7. Inflation*

   a. Decision process tool   b. Cost of living
   c. Bear raid   d. Restructuring

13. _____ is a United States military entitlement given to military servicemen and women living in high cost areas or stationed overseas. It is intended to compensate servicemembers for the high cost of living at certain duty stations.

The fundamental goal of _____ is to compensate servicemembers for the high cost of living at certain duty stations.

   a. 100-year flood   b. 130-30 fund
   c. Cost of Living Allowance   d. 1921 recession

14. _____ is a fee paid on borrowed assets. It is the price paid for the use of borrowed money, or, money earned by deposited funds. Assets that are sometimes lent with _____ include money, shares, consumer goods through hire purchase, major assets such as aircraft, and even entire factories in finance lease arrangements.

   a. Asset protection   b. Interest
   c. Insolvency   d. Internal debt

15. An _____ is the price a borrower pays for the use of money they do not own, for instance a small company might borrow from a bank to kick start their business, and the return a lender receives for deferring the use of funds, by lending it to the borrower. _____s are normally expressed as a percentage rate over the period of one year.

_____s targets are also a vital tool of monetary policy and are used to control variables like investment, inflation, and unemployment.

   a. Enterprise value   b. Arrow-Debreu model
   c. ACCRA Cost of Living Index   d. Interest rate

16. A security is a fungible, negotiable instrument representing financial value. _____ are broadly categorized into debt _____; equity _____, e.g., common stocks; and derivative (finance) contracts such as forwards, futures, options and swaps. The company or other entity issuing the security is called the issuer.

   a. Settlement risk   b. Pass-Through Certificates
   c. Red herring prospectus   d. Securities

17. _____ are the inflation-indexed bonds issued by the U.S. Treasury. The principal is adjusted to the Consumer Price Index, the commonly used measure of inflation. The coupon rate is constant, but generates a different amount of interest when multiplied by the inflation-adjusted principal, thus protecting the holder against inflation.

   a. 1921 recession   b. 130-30 fund
   c. Treasury Inflation-Protected Securities   d. 100-year flood

18. _____ is a broad label that refers to any individuals or households that use goods and services generated within the economy. The concept of a _____ is used in different contexts, so that the usage and significance of the term may vary.

Chapter 7. Inflation 43

Typically when business people and economists talk of _____s they are talking about person as _____, an aggregated commodity item with little individuality other than that expressed in the buy/not-buy decision.

a. 1921 recession
c. Consumer

b. 100-year flood
d. 130-30 fund

19. A _____ is a measure of the average price of consumer goods and services purchased by households. A _____ measures a price change for a constant market basket of goods and services from one period to the next within the same area (city, region, or nation.) It is a price index determined by measuring the price of a standard group of goods meant to represent the typical market basket of a typical urban consumer.

a. Lipstick index
c. CPI

b. Cost-of-living index
d. Consumer price index

20. A _____ is a normalized average (typically a weighted average) of prices for a given class of goods or services in a given region, during a given interval of time. It is a statistic designed to help to compare how these prices, taken as a whole, differ between time periods or geographical locations.

Price indices have several potential uses.

a. Transactional Net Margin Method
c. Product sabotage

b. Two-part tariff
d. Price index

21. A _____ measures average changes in prices received by domestic producers for their output. It is one of several price indices

Its importance is being undermined by the steady decline in manufactured goods as a share of spending.

A number of countries that now report a _____ previously reported a Wholesale Price Index.

a. Producer price index
c. Hemline index

b. Visible balance
d. Gross national product

22. The term _____ or commodity bundle refers to a fixed list of items used specifically to track the progress of inflation in an economy or specific market.

The most common type of _____ is the basket of consumer goods, used to define the Consumer Price Index (CPI.) Other types of baskets are used to define

- Producer Price Index (PPI), previously known as Wholesale Price Index (WPI)
- various commodity price indices

Chapter 7. Inflation

The term _____ analysis in the retail business refers to research that provides the retailer with information to understand the purchase behaviour of a buyer. This information will enable the retailer to understand the buyer's needs and rewrite the store's layout accordingly, develop cross-promotional programs, or even capture new buyers (much like the cross-selling concept.)

    a. Category Development Index
    b. Cost-weighted activity index
    c. Robin Hood index
    d. Market basket

23. In economics, _____ refers to any price or value expressed in money of the day, as opposed to real value, which adjusts for the effect of inflation. Examples include a bundle of commodities, such as gross domestic product, and income. For a series of _____ s in successive years, different values could be because of differences in the price level, an index of prices.

    a. Financial crisis
    b. Treasury View
    c. Nominal value
    d. Tobit model

24. _____ is the a method of technical and economic research of the systems for purpose to optimize a parity between system's consumer functions or properties and expenses to achieve those functions or properties.

This methodology for continuous perfection of production, industrial technologies, organizational structures was developed by Juryj Sobolev in 1948 at the 'Perm telephone factory'

- 1948 Juryj Sobolev - the first success in application of a method analysis at the 'Perm telephone factory' .
- 1949 - the first application for the invention as result of use of the new method.

Today in economically developed countries practically each enterprise or the company use methodology of the kind of functional-cost analysis as a practice of the quality management, most full satisfying to principles of standards of series ISO 9000.

- Interest of consumer not in products itself, but the advantage which it will receive from its usage.
- The consumer aspires to reduce his expenses
- Functions needed by consumer can be executed in the various ways, and, hence, with various efficiency and expenses. Among possible alternatives of realization of functions exist such in which the parity of quality and the price is the optimal for the consumer.

The goal of _____ is achievement of the highest consumer satisfaction of production at simultaneous decrease in all kinds of industrial expenses Classical _____ has three English synonyms - Value Engineering, Value Management, Value Analysis.

    a. Function cost analysis
    b. Monopoly wage
    c. Willingness to pay
    d. Staple financing

Chapter 7. Inflation

25. In finance and economics _____ or nominal rate of interest refers to the rate of interest before adjustment for inflation (in contrast with the real interest rate); or, for interest rates 'as stated' without adjustment for the full effect of compounding (also referred to as the nominal annual rate.) An interest rate is called nominal if the frequency of compounding (e.g. a month) is not identical to the basic time unit (normally a year.)

The real interest rate includes compensation for the lender's lost value due to inflation, whereas the _____ excludes inflation.

   a. Risk-free interest rate
   b. Fixed interest
   c. Nominal interest rate
   d. London Interbank Offered Rate

26. The '_____' is approximately the nominal interest rate minus the inflation rate Since the inflation rate over the course of a loan is not known initially, volatility in inflation represents a risk to both the lender and the borrower.

In economics and finance, an individual who lends money for repayment at a later point in time expects to be compensated for the time value of money, or not having the use of that money while it is lent.

   a. Cost-push inflation
   b. Core inflation
   c. Reflation
   d. Real interest rate

27. A _____ is the price of a representative basket of wholesale goods. Some countries (like India and The Philippines) use _____ changes as a central measure of inflation. However, India and the United States now report a producer price index instead.
   a. TED spread
   b. Producer Price Index
   c. Lagging indicator
   d. Wholesale price index

28. A _____ is the lowest hourly, daily or monthly wage that employers may legally pay to employees or workers. Equivalently, it is the lowest wage at which workers may sell their labor. Although _____ laws are in effect in a great many jurisdictions, there are differences of opinion about the benefits and drawbacks of a _____.
   a. Permanent war economy
   b. Marginal propensity to consume
   c. Microfoundations
   d. Minimum wage

29. An _____, in economics, is the amount by which the real Gross domestic product exceeds potential GDP. The real GDP is also known as GDP 'adjusted for inflation', 'constant prices' GDP or 'constant dollar' GDP, because it measures the aggregate output in a country's income accounts in a given year, expressed in base-year prices. On the other hand, the potential GDP is the quantity of real GDP when a country's economy is at full-employment.
   a. ACEA agreement
   b. AD-IA Model
   c. ACCRA Cost of Living Index
   d. Inflationary gap

30. _____ describes a bias in gay economics index numbers arising from tendency to purchase inexpensive substitutes for expensive items when prices change.

_____ occurs when two or more items experience a change of price relative to each other. Consumers will consume more of the now comparatively inexpensive good and less of the now relatively more expensive good.

a. State of World Liberty Index
b. Market basket
c. Constant dollars
d. Substitution bias

31. _____ is a term used to described a tendency or preference towards a particular perspective, ideology or result, especially when the tendency interferes with the ability to be impartial, unprejudiced, or objective. The term _____ed is used to describe an action, judgment, or other outcome influenced by a prejudged perspective. It is also used to refer to a person or body of people whose actions or judgments exhibit _____.
    a. Bias
    b. 130-30 fund
    c. 100-year flood
    d. 1921 recession

32. In economics, _____ is inflation that is very high or 'out of control', a condition in which prices increase rapidly as a currency loses its value. Definitions used by the media vary from a cumulative inflation rate over three years approaching 100% to 'inflation exceeding 50% a month.' In informal usage the term is often applied to much lower rates. As a rule of thumb, normal inflation is reported per year, but _____ is often reported for much shorter intervals, often per month.
    a. 1921 recession
    b. 100-year flood
    c. 130-30 fund
    d. Hyperinflation

33. In economics, _____, also hedonic demand theory, is a method of estimating demand or value. It decomposes the item being researched into its constituent characteristics, and obtains estimates of the contributory value of each characteristic. This requires that the composite good being valued can be reduced to its constituent parts and that the market values those constituent parts.
    a. Future interest
    b. Foreclosure investment
    c. Hedonic regression
    d. Family farm

34. A _____ is:

- Rewrite _____, in generative grammar and computer science
- Standardization, a formal and widely-accepted statement, fact, definition, or qualification
- Operation, a determinate _____ for performing a mathematical operation and obtaining a certain result (Mathematics, Logic)
    - Unary operation
    - Binary operation
- _____ of inference, a function from sets of formulae to formulae (Mathematics, Logic)
- _____ of thumb, principle with broad application that is not intended to be strictly accurate or reliable for every situation. Also often simply referred to as a _____
- Moral, an atomic element of a moral code for guiding choices in human behavior
- Heuristic, a quantized '_____' which shows a tendency or probability for successful function
- A regulation, as in sports
- A Production _____, as in computer science
- Procedural law, a _____ set governing the application of laws to cases
    - A law, which may informally be called a '_____'
    - A court ruling, a decision by a court
- In the U.S. Government, a regulation mandated by Congress, but written or expanded upon by the Executive Branch.
- Norm (sociology), an informal but widely accepted _____, concept, truth, definition, or qualification (social norms, legal norms, coding norms)
- Norm (philosophy), a kind of sentence or a reason to act, feel or believe
- 'Rulership' is the concept of governance by a government:
    - Military _____, governance by a military body
    - Monastic _____, a collection of precepts that guides the life of monks or nuns in a religious order where the superior holds the place of Christ
- Slide _____

- '_____,' a song by Ayumi Hamasaki
- '_____,' a song by rapper Nas
- '_____s,' an album by the band The Whitest Boy Alive
- _____s: Pyaar Ka Superhit Formula, a 2003 Bollywood film
- ruler, an instrument for measuring lengths
- _____, a component of an astrolabe, circumferator or similar instrument
- The _____s, a bestselling self-help book
- _____ Project (Run Up-to-date Linux Everywhere), a project that aims to use up-to-date Linux software on old PCs
- _____ engine, a software system that helps managing business _____s
- Ja _____, a hip hop artist
    - R.U.L.E., a 2005 greatest hits album by rapper Ja _____
- '_____s,' a KMFDM song

a. Procter ' Gamble   b. Technocracy
c. Demand   d. Rule

Chapter 8. A Framework for Macroeconomic Analysis

1. In economics, _____ is the total demand for final goods and services in the economy (Y) at a given time and price level. It is the amount of goods and services in the economy that will be purchased at all possible price levels. This is the demand for the gross domestic product of a country when inventory levels are static.
   - a. Aggregate supply
   - b. Aggregation problem
   - c. Aggregate expenditure
   - d. Aggregate demand

2. In economics, _____ is the total supply of goods and services produced by a national economy during a specific time period. It is the total amount of goods and services in the economy available at all possible price levels.
   - a. Aggregation problem
   - b. Aggregate demand
   - c. Aggregate expenditure
   - d. Aggregate supply

3. Economics:

   - _____, the desire to own something and the ability to pay for it
   - _____ curve, a graphic representation of a _____ schedule
   - _____ deposit, the money in checking accounts
   - _____ pull theory, the theory that inflation occurs when _____ for goods and services exceeds existing supplies
   - _____ schedule, a table that lists the quantity of a good a person will buy it each different price
   - _____ side economics, the school of economics at believes government spending and tax cuts open economy by raising _____

   - a. Variability
   - b. Production
   - c. McKesson ' Robbins scandal
   - d. Demand

4. _____ is a branch of economics that deals with the performance, structure, and behavior of a national or regional economy as a whole. Along with microeconomics, _____ is one of the two most general fields in economics. It is the study of the behavior and decision-making of entire economies.
   - a. Macroeconomics
   - b. Nominal value
   - c. Tobit model
   - d. New Trade Theory

5. _____ is a branch of economics that studies how individuals, households and firms and some states make decisions to allocate limited resources, typically in markets where goods or services are being bought and sold. _____ examines how these decisions and behaviours affect the supply and demand for goods and services, which determines prices; and how prices, in turn, determine the supply and demand of goods and services.

   Whereas macroeconomics involves the 'sum total of economic activity, dealing with the issues of growth, inflation and unemployment, and with national economic policies relating to these issues' and the effects of government actions on them.

   - a. Countercyclical
   - b. Recession
   - c. Microeconomics
   - d. New Keynesian economics

6. _____ is widely regarded as the first modern school of economic thought. It is the idea that free markets can regulate themselves. Its major developers include Adam Smith, David Ricardo, Thomas Malthus and John Stuart Mill. Sometimes the definition of _____ is expanded to include William Petty, Johann Heinrich von Thünen.

a. Schools of economic thought
b. Tendency of the rate of profit to fall
c. Marginalism
d. Classical economics

7. In macroeconomics, _____ is a condition of the national economy, where all or nearly all persons willing and able to work at the prevailing wages and working conditions are able to do so. It is defined either as 0% unemployment, literally, no unemployment (the rate of unemployment is the fraction of the work force unable to find work), as by James Tobin, or as the level of employment rates when there is no cyclical unemployment. It is defined by the majority of mainstream economists as being an acceptable level of natural unemployment above 0%, the discrepancy from 0% being due to non-cyclical types of unemployment.
   a. Marginal propensity to consume
   b. Full employment
   c. Demand shock
   d. Harrod-Johnson diagram

8. _____, 1st Baron Keynes was a renowned economist from Britain whose many ideas on economic and political theories as well as on many governments' monetary policies influenced America. He advocated a government that played an active role in the lives of people regarding business, economy, etc. In this role, the government would use fiscal measures to reduce the consequences of recessions, economic depressions and booms.
   a. Adolf Hitler
   b. Adam Smith
   c. Adolph Fischer
   d. John Maynard Keynes

9. _____ and Keynesian Theory) is a macroeconomic theory based on the ideas of 20th-century British economist John Maynard Keynes. _____ argues that private sector decisions sometimes lead to inefficient macroeconomic outcomes and therefore advocates active policy responses by the public sector, including monetary policy actions by the central bank and fiscal policy actions by the government to stabilize output over the business cycle.

The theories forming the basis of _____ were first presented in The General Theory of Employment, Interest and Money, published in 1936.

   a. Rational choice theory
   b. Market failure
   c. Deflation
   d. Keynesian economics

10. _____s is the social science that studies the production, distribution, and consumption of goods and services. The term _____s comes from the Ancient Greek oἰκονομία from oἶκος (oikos, 'house') + νόμος (nomos, 'custom' or 'law'), hence 'rules of the house(hold)'. Current _____ models developed out of the broader field of political economy in the late 19th century, owing to a desire to use an empirical approach more akin to the physical sciences.
   a. Energy economics
   b. Opportunity cost
   c. Inflation
   d. Economic

11. A _____ is the space, actual or metaphorical, in which a market operates. The term is also used in a trademark law context to denote the actual consumer environment, ie. the 'real world' in which products and services are provided and consumed.
   a. 1921 recession
   b. Marketplace
   c. 100-year flood
   d. 130-30 fund

12. _____ was a survey conducted by the U.S. Department of Justice to gauge the prevalence of alcohol and illegal drug use among prior arrestees. It was a reformulation of the prior Drug Use Forecasting (DUF) program, focused on five drugs in particular: cocaine, marijuana, methamphetamine, opiates, and PCP.

50   *Chapter 8. A Framework for Macroeconomic Analysis*

Participants were randomly selected from arrest records in major metropolitan areas; because no personally identifying information is taken from each record chosen, the resulting data can be correlated to arrest rates, but not to the total population of persons charged.

  a. ACCRA Cost of Living Index
  b. AD-IA Model
  c. Arrestee Drug Abuse Monitoring
  d. ACEA agreement

13. _____ was a Scottish moral philosopher and a pioneer of political economy. One of the key figures of the Scottish Enlightenment, Smith is the author of The Theory of Moral Sentiments and An Inquiry into the Nature and Causes of the Wealth of Nations. The latter, usually abbreviated as The Wealth of Nations, is considered his magnum opus and the first modern work of economics.
  a. Adolf Hitler
  b. Adam Smith
  c. Alan Greenspan
  d. Adolph Fischer

14. An Inquiry into the Nature and Causes of the _____ is the magnum opus of the Scottish economist Adam Smith. It is a clearly written account of economics at the dawn of the Industrial Revolution, as well as a rhetorical piece written for the generally educated individual of the 18th century - advocating a free market economy as more productive and more beneficial to society.

The work is credited as a watershed in history and economics due to its comprehensive, largely accurate characterization of economic mechanisms that survive in modern economics; and also for its effective use of rhetorical technique, including structuring the work to contrast real world examples of free and fettered markets.

  a. Wealth of Nations
  b. The Bell Curve
  c. The Rise and Fall of the Great Powers
  d. Black Book of Communism

15. _____ refers to a business or organization attempting to acquire goods or services to accomplish the goals of the enterprise. Though there are several organizations that attempt to set standards in the _____ process, processes can vary greatly between organizations. Typically the word '_____' is not used interchangeably with the word 'procurement', since procurement typically includes Expediting, Supplier Quality, and Traffic and Logistics (T'L) in addition to _____.
  a. 130-30 fund
  b. 100-year flood
  c. Purchasing
  d. Free port

16. _____ is the number of goods/services that can be purchased with a unit of currency. For example, if you had taken one dollar to a store in the 1950s, you would have been able to buy a greater number of items than you would today, indicating that you would have had a greater _____ in the 1950s. Currency can be either a commodity money, like gold or silver, or fiat currency like US dollars.
  a. Human Poverty Index
  b. Compliance cost
  c. Genuine progress indicator
  d. Purchasing power

17. The _____ is an economic term, referring to an increase in spending that accompanies an increase or perceived increase in wealth.

The effect would cause changes in the amounts and composition of consumer consumption caused by changes in consumer wealth. People should spend more when one of two things is true: when people actually are richer (by objective measurement, for example, a bonus or a pay raise at work, which would be an income effect), or when people perceive themselves to be 'richer' (for example, the assessed value of their home increases, or a stock they own has gone up in price recently.)

a. Wealth effect
b. 130-30 fund
c. Wealth condensation
d. 100-year flood

18. The _____ or gross domestic income (GDI), a basic measure of an economy's economic performance, is the market value of all final goods and services produced within the borders of a nation in a year. _____ can be defined in three ways, all of which are conceptually identical. First, it is equal to the total expenditures for all final goods and services produced within the country in a stipulated period of time (usually a 365-day year.)

a. Monopolistic competition
b. Market structure
c. Countercyclical
d. Gross domestic product

19. In economic models, the _____ time frame assumes no fixed factors of production. Firms can enter or leave the marketplace, and the cost (and availability) of land, labor, raw materials, and capital goods can be assumed to vary. In contrast, in the short-run time frame, certain factors are assumed to be fixed, because there is not sufficient time for them to change.

a. Productivity world
b. Price/performance ratio
c. Diseconomies of scale
d. Long-run

20. In economics, the concept of the _____ refers to the decision-making time frame of a firm in which at least one factor of production is fixed. Costs which are fixed in the _____ have no impact on a firms decisions. For example a firm can raise output by increasing the amount of labour through overtime.

a. Product Pipeline
b. Productivity model
c. Hicks-neutral technical change
d. Short-run

21. _____ in economics and business is the result of an exchange and from that trade we assign a numerical monetary value to a good, service or asset. If Alice trades Bob 4 apples for an orange, the _____ of an orange is 4 apples. Inversely, the _____ of an apple is 1/4 oranges.

a. Price war
b. Premium pricing
c. Price book
d. Price

22. The Demand side is a term used in economics to refer to a number of things:

- The demand element of a supply and demand partial equilibrium diagram, in microeconomics
- The aggregate demand in an economy, in macroeconomics
- Economic policy actions which are designed to affect aggregate demand.
- _____ learning referring to the incentive to learn how to use and modify free software as opposed to buying conventional software.

The term is also used broadly to distinguish supply-side economics from other schools, for instance Keynesian economics.

Chapter 8. A Framework for Macroeconomic Analysis

a. Delayed differentiation
c. Reverse auction
b. Demand-side
d. CPFR

23. _____ Theory (or _____ Theory) is a class of macroeconomic models in which business cycle fluctuations to a large extent can be accounted for by real (in contrast to nominal) shocks. (The four primary economic fluctuations are secular (trend), business cycle, seasonal, and random.) Unlike other leading theories of the business cycle, it sees recessions and periods of economic growth as the efficient response to exogenous changes in the real economic environment.

a. SIMIC
c. Real business cycle
b. Balanced-growth equilibrium
d. Monetary policy reaction function

24. A _____ is an event that suddenly changes the price of a commodity or service. It may be caused by a sudden increase or decrease in the supply of a particular good. This sudden change affects the equilibrium price.

a. Friedman rule
c. Supply shock
b. Demand shock
d. SIMIC

25. _____ is a school of macroeconomic thought that argues that economic growth can be most effectively created using incentives for people to produce (supply) goods and services, such as adjusting income tax and capital gains tax rates, and by allowing greater flexibility by reducing regulation. Consumers will then benefit from a greater supply of goods and services at lower prices.

The term _____ was coined by journalist Jude Wanniski in 1975, and popularized the ideas of economists Robert Mundell and Arthur Laffer.

a. Commodity trading advisors
c. Clap note
b. Supply-side economics
d. Fiscal stimulus plans

26. The term _____ refers to economy-wide fluctuations in production or economic activity over several months or years. These fluctuations occur around a long-term growth trend, and typically involve shifts over time between periods of relatively rapid economic growth (expansion or boom), and periods of relative stagnation or decline (contraction or recession.)

These fluctuations are often measured using the growth rate of real gross domestic product.

a. Business cycle
c. Tobit model
b. Nominal value
d. Consumer theory

27. Necessary _____ s:

If x is a necessary _____ of y, then the presence of y necessarily implies the presence of x. The presence of x, however, does not imply that y will occur.

Sufficient _____ s:

If x is a sufficient _____ of y, then the presence of x necessarily implies the presence of y.

a. Political philosophy
b. Philosophy of economics
c. Materialism
d. Cause

28.　In economics, _____ is a sustained decrease in the general price level of goods and services. _____ occurs when the annual inflation rate falls below zero percent, resulting in an increase in the real value of money -- a negative inflation rate. This should not be confused with disinflation, a slow-down in the inflation rate (i.e. when the inflation decreases, but still remains positive.)
　　a. Literacy rate
　　b. Tobit model
　　c. Price revolution
　　d. Deflation

29.　In economics, _____ is a rise in the general level of prices of goods and services in an economy over a period of time. When the general price level rises, each unit of currency buys fewer goods and services; consequently, _____ is also a decline in the real value of money--a loss of purchasing power in the medium of exchange which is also the monetary unit of account in the economy. A chief measure of general price-level _____ is the general _____ rate, which is the percentage change in a general price index (normally the Consumer Price Index) over time.
　　a. Opportunity cost
　　b. Economic
　　c. Energy economics
　　d. Inflation

Chapter 9. Fiscal Policy and Short-Run Instability

1. The term _____ refers to economy-wide fluctuations in production or economic activity over several months or years. These fluctuations occur around a long-term growth trend, and typically involve shifts over time between periods of relatively rapid economic growth (expansion or boom), and periods of relative stagnation or decline (contraction or recession.)

These fluctuations are often measured using the growth rate of real gross domestic product.

   a. Consumer theory
   b. Nominal value
   c. Tobit model
   d. Business cycle

2. The term _____ refers to government debt, expenditures and revenues, or to finance (particularly financial revenue) in general.

   - _____ deficit is the budget deficit of federal or local government
   - _____ policy is the discretionary spending of governments. Contrasts with monetary policy.
   - _____ year and _____ quarter are reporting periods for firms and other agencies.

   a. Drawdown
   b. Bucket shop
   c. Procter ' Gamble
   d. Fiscal

3. In economics, _____ is the use of government spending and revenue collection to influence the economy.

   _____ can be contrasted with the other main type of economic policy, monetary policy, which attempts to stabilize the economy by controlling interest rates and the supply of money. The two main instruments of _____ are government spending and taxation.

   a. Sustainable investment rule
   b. Fiscalism
   c. Fiscal policy
   d. 100-year flood

4. _____ and Keynesian Theory) is a macroeconomic theory based on the ideas of 20th-century British economist John Maynard Keynes. _____ argues that private sector decisions sometimes lead to inefficient macroeconomic outcomes and therefore advocates active policy responses by the public sector, including monetary policy actions by the central bank and fiscal policy actions by the government to stabilize output over the business cycle.

   The theories forming the basis of _____ were first presented in The General Theory of Employment, Interest and Money, published in 1936.

   a. Rational choice theory
   b. Keynesian economics
   c. Deflation
   d. Market failure

5. _____s is the social science that studies the production, distribution, and consumption of goods and services. The term _____s comes from the Ancient Greek oá¼°κονομῖα from oá¼¶κος (oikos, 'house') + vÏŒμος (nomos, 'custom' or 'law'), hence 'rules of the house(hold)'. Current _____ models developed out of the broader field of political economy in the late 19th century, owing to a desire to use an empirical approach more akin to the physical sciences.

Chapter 9. Fiscal Policy and Short-Run Instability

a. Energy economics
c. Opportunity cost
b. Inflation
d. Economic

6. _____ refers to the process where tax thresholds are either not adjusted for inflation causing in either case an automatic rise in tax revenues.

Suppose a person earns $20,000 per year and is liable to 20% tax on earnings above a threshold of $5,000 per year. Then they pay (20000-5000)*0.2 = $3000 in tax, or 15% of income.

a. Tax sale
c. Tax law
b. Taxation as slavery
d. Fiscal drag

7. In economics, the _____ or spending multiplier is the idea that an initial amount of spending (usually by the government) leads to increased consumption spending and so results in an increase in national income greater than the initial amount of spending. In other words, an initial change in aggregate demand causes a change in aggregate output for the economy that is a multiple of the initial change.

The existence of a _____ was initially proposed by Ralph George Hawtrey in 1931.

a. Keynesian cross
c. Magical triangle
b. Spending multiplier
d. Multiplier effect

8. The GDP gap or the _____ is the difference between potential GDP and actual GDP or actual output. The calculation for the _____ is Y-Y* where Y* is potential output and Y is actual output. If this calculation yields a positive number it is called an expansionary gap and indicates an economy in expansion; if the calculation yields a negative number it is called a recessionary gap and indicates an economy in recession.

a. ACEA agreement
c. AD-IA Model
b. ACCRA Cost of Living Index
d. Output gap

9. The GDP gap or the output gap is the difference between potential GDP and actual GDP or actual output. The calculation for the output gap is Y-Y* where Y* is potential output and Y is actual output. If this calculation yields a positive number it is called an expansionary gap and indicates an economy in expansion; if the calculation yields a negative number it is called a _____ and indicates an economy in recession.

a. 130-30 fund
c. 1921 recession
b. 100-year flood
d. Recessionary gap

10. An _____, in economics, is the amount by which the real Gross domestic product exceeds potential GDP. The real GDP is also known as GDP 'adjusted for inflation', 'constant prices' GDP or 'constant dollar' GDP, because it measures the aggregate output in a country's income accounts in a given year, expressed in base-year prices. On the other hand, the potential GDP is the quantity of real GDP when a country's economy is at full-employment.

a. ACCRA Cost of Living Index
c. AD-IA Model
b. ACEA agreement
d. Inflationary gap

11. In economic models, the _____ time frame assumes no fixed factors of production. Firms can enter or leave the marketplace, and the cost (and availability) of land, labor, raw materials, and capital goods can be assumed to vary. In contrast, in the short-run time frame, certain factors are assumed to be fixed, because there is not sufficient time for them to change.
  a. Long-run
  b. Diseconomies of scale
  c. Price/performance ratio
  d. Productivity world

12. In economics, _____ is the total supply of goods and services produced by a national economy during a specific time period. It is the total amount of goods and services in the economy available at all possible price levels.
  a. Aggregate expenditure
  b. Aggregation problem
  c. Aggregate demand
  d. Aggregate supply

13. _____ is a common concept in economics, and gives rise to derived concepts such as consumer debt. Generally _____ is defined by opposition to production. But the precise definition can vary because different schools of economists define production quite differently.
  a. Federal Reserve Bank Notes
  b. Consumption
  c. Foreclosure data providers
  d. Cash or share options

14. From a Keynesian point of view, a _____ in the public sector is achieved when the government equates the revenues with expenditure over the business cycles. In other words, a government's budget is balanced if its income is equal to its expenditure. It is a budget in which revenues are equal to spending.
  a. Budget theory
  b. Budget support
  c. Budget crisis
  d. Balanced budget

15. A _____ occurs when an entity spends more money than it takes in. The opposite of a _____ is a budget surplus. Debt is essentially an accumulated flow of deficits.
  a. Funding body
  b. Public Financial Management
  c. Lump-sum tax
  d. Budget deficit

16. A _____ is a situation in which the government takes in more than it spends.
  a. 130-30 fund
  b. Budget surplus
  c. 100-year flood
  d. Budget set

17. _____ forms part of the public sector deficit. _____ differs from cyclical deficit in that it exists even when the economy is at its potential.

_____ issues can only be addressed by explicit and direct government policies: reducing spending (including entitlements), increasing the tax base, and/or increasing tax rates.

  a. Sovereign credit
  b. Structural deficit
  c. Tax increment financing
  d. Minimum Municipal Obligation

18. _____ is that which is owed; usually referencing assets owed, but the term can also cover moral obligations and other interactions not requiring money. In the case of assets, _____ is a means of using future purchasing power in the present before a summation has been earned. Some companies and corporations use _____ as a part of their overall corporate finance strategy.

Chapter 9. Fiscal Policy and Short-Run Instability

a. Collateral Management
b. Debenture
c. Hard money loan
d. Debt

19. _____ is a term used to describe macroeconomic policy based on the ad hoc judgment of policymakers as opposed to policy set by predetermined rules. For instance, a central banker could make decisions on interest rates on a case by case basis instead of allowing a set rule, such as the Taylor rule, determine interest rates.

Discretionary policies are similar to 'feedback-rule policies' used by the Federal Reserve to achieve price level stability.

a. Discretionary policy
b. Managerial economics
c. Demand for money
d. Boom and bust

20. The _____ or gross domestic income (GDI), a basic measure of an economy's economic performance, is the market value of all final goods and services produced within the borders of a nation in a year. _____ can be defined in three ways, all of which are conceptually identical. First, it is equal to the total expenditures for all final goods and services produced within the country in a stipulated period of time (usually a 365-day year.)

a. Monopolistic competition
b. Gross domestic product
c. Countercyclical
d. Market structure

21. In economics, _____ is the total demand for final goods and services in the economy (Y) at a given time and price level. It is the amount of goods and services in the economy that will be purchased at all possible price levels. This is the demand for the gross domestic product of a country when inventory levels are static.

a. Aggregate expenditure
b. Aggregate supply
c. Aggregation problem
d. Aggregate demand

22. Economics:

- _____, the desire to own something and the ability to pay for it
- _____ curve, a graphic representation of a _____ schedule
- _____ deposit, the money in checking accounts
- _____ pull theory, the theory that inflation occurs when _____ for goods and services exceeds existing supplies
- _____ schedule, a table that lists the quantity of a good a person will buy it each different price
- _____ side economics, the school of economics at believes government spending and tax cuts open economy by raising _____

a. Variability
b. Demand
c. Production
d. McKesson ' Robbins scandal

23. In economics, the concept of the _____ refers to the decision-making time frame of a firm in which at least one factor of production is fixed. Costs which are fixed in the _____ have no impact on a firms decisions. For example a firm can raise output by increasing the amount of labour through overtime.

a. Product Pipeline
b. Productivity model
c. Short-run
d. Hicks-neutral technical change

24. In microeconomics, _____ is quite simply the conversion of inputs into outputs. It is an economic process that uses resources to create a good or service that is suitable for exchange. This can include manufacturing, storing, shipping, and packaging.
    a. Solved
    b. Production
    c. Red Guards
    d. MET

25. _____ arises when aggregate demand in an economy outpaces aggregate supply. It involves inflation rising as real gross domestic product rises and unemployment falls, as the economy moves along the Phillips curve. This is commonly described as 'too much money chasing too few goods'.
    a. Marshallian demand function
    b. Demand-pull inflation
    c. Kinked demand
    d. Kinked demand curve

26. In economics, _____ is a rise in the general level of prices of goods and services in an economy over a period of time. When the general price level rises, each unit of currency buys fewer goods and services; consequently, _____ is also a decline in the real value of money--a loss of purchasing power in the medium of exchange which is also the monetary unit of account in the economy. A chief measure of general price-level _____ is the general _____ rate, which is the percentage change in a general price index (normally the Consumer Price Index) over time.
    a. Economic
    b. Inflation
    c. Energy economics
    d. Opportunity cost

27. _____ is a type of inflation caused by substantial increases in the cost of important goods or services where no suitable alternative is available. A situation that has been often cited of this was the oil crisis of the 1970s, which some economists see as a major cause of the inflation experienced in the Western world in that decade. It is argued that this inflation resulted from increases in the cost of petroleum imposed by the member states of OPEC.
    a. Mundell-Tobin effect
    b. Headline inflation
    c. Chronic inflation
    d. Cost-push inflation

28. _____ is an economic situation in which inflation and economic stagnation occur simultaneously and remain unchecked for a period of time. The portmanteau _____ is generally attributed to British politician Iain Macleod, who coined the term in a speech to Parliament in 1965. The concept is notable partly because, in postwar macroeconomic theory, inflation and recession were regarded as mutually exclusive, and also because _____ has generally proven to be difficult and costly to eradicate once it gets started.
    a. Chronic inflation
    b. Real interest rate
    c. Stagflation
    d. Price/wage spiral

29. In economics, _____ means that people form their expectations about what will happen in the future based on what has happened in the past. For example, if inflation has been higher than expected in the past, people would revise expectations for the future.

One simple version of _____ is stated in the following equation, where p^e is the next year's rate of inflation that is currently expected; p^e_{-1} is this year's rate of inflation that was expected last year; and p is this year's actual rate of inflation:

$$p^e = p^e_{-1} + \lambda(p_{-1} - p^e_{-1})$$

With λ is between 0 and 1, this says that current expectations of future inflation reflect past expectations and an 'error-adjustment' term, in which current expectations are raised (or lowered) according to the gap between actual inflation and previous expectations.

a. Adaptive expectations
b. Economic interdependence
c. AD-IA Model
d. Investment-specific technological progress

30. In economics, the _____ is a historical inverse relation between the rate of unemployment and the rate of inflation in an economy. Stated simply, the lower the unemployment in an economy, the higher the rate of increase in nominal wages in the economy. Rate of Change of Wages against Unemployment, United Kingdom 1913-1948 from Phillips (1958)

William Phillips, a New Zealand born economist, wrote a paper in 1958 titled The Relationship between Unemployment and the Rate of Change of Money Wages in the United Kingdom 1861-1957, which was published in the quarterly journal Economica.

a. Phillips curve
b. Lorenz curve
c. Cost curve
d. Demand curve

31. _____ is an assumption used in many contemporary macroeconomic models, and also in other areas of contemporary economics and game theory and in other applications of rational choice theory.

Since most macroeconomic models today study decisions over many periods, the expectations of workers, consumers, and firms about future economic conditions are an essential part of the model. How to model these expectations has long been controversial, and it is well known that the macroeconomic predictions of the model may differ depending on the assumptions made about expectations

a. Balanced-growth equilibrium
b. Minimum wage
c. Potential output
d. Rational expectations

32. _____ is widely regarded as the first modern school of economic thought. It is the idea that free markets can regulate themselves. Its major developers include Adam Smith, David Ricardo, Thomas Malthus and John Stuart Mill. Sometimes the definition of _____ is expanded to include William Petty, Johann Heinrich von Thünen.

a. Tendency of the rate of profit to fall
b. Marginalism
c. Classical economics
d. Schools of economic thought

33. The balance of trade (or net exports, sometimes symbolized as NX) is the difference between the monetary value of exports and imports in an economy over a certain period of time. It is the relationship between a nation's imports and exports. A favorable balance of trade is known as a trade surplus and consists of exporting more than is imported; an unfavorable balance of trade is known as a _____ or, informally, a trade gap.

   a. Trade deficit
   b. Complementary asset
   c. Computational economic
   d. Demographics of India

34. The _____ hypothesis is a concept from macroeconomics that contends that there is a strong link between a national economy's current account balance and its government budget balance. As an example, it is hypothesized that a large budget deficit leads to a large current account deficit. The theory goes as follows:

$$Y = C + I + G + NX$$

where Y represents National Income or GDP, C is consumption, I is investment, G is government spending and NX stands for net exports.

   a. Twin deficits
   b. 100-year flood
   c. Power of the purse
   d. Public-private partnership

Chapter 10. Aggregate Expenditures

1. In economics, _____ is a measure of national income. Basically, it is an approach to measure GDP. It is defined as the value of planned goods and services produced in an economy.
   a. Aggregate supply
   b. Aggregation problem
   c. Aggregate demand
   d. Aggregate expenditure

2. _____ is widely regarded as the first modern school of economic thought. It is the idea that free markets can regulate themselves.Its major developers include Adam Smith, David Ricardo, Thomas Malthus and John Stuart Mill. Sometimes the definition of _____ is expanded to include William Petty, Johann Heinrich von Thünen.
   a. Tendency of the rate of profit to fall
   b. Marginalism
   c. Schools of economic thought
   d. Classical economics

3. _____, 1st Baron Keynes was a renowned economist from Britain whose many ideas on economic and political theories as well as on many governments' monetary policies influenced America. He advocated a government that played an active role in the lives of people regarding business, economy, etc. In this role, the government would use fiscal measures to reduce the consequences of recessions, economic depressions and booms.
   a. Adolf Hitler
   b. Adam Smith
   c. Adolph Fischer
   d. John Maynard Keynes

4. _____ and Keynesian Theory) is a macroeconomic theory based on the ideas of 20th-century British economist John Maynard Keynes. _____ argues that private sector decisions sometimes lead to inefficient macroeconomic outcomes and therefore advocates active policy responses by the public sector, including monetary policy actions by the central bank and fiscal policy actions by the government to stabilize output over the business cycle.

   The theories forming the basis of _____ were first presented in The General Theory of Employment, Interest and Money, published in 1936.

   a. Rational choice theory
   b. Deflation
   c. Market failure
   d. Keynesian economics

5. _____s is the social science that studies the production, distribution, and consumption of goods and services. The term _____s comes from the Ancient Greek oá¼°κονομῖα from oá¼¶κος (oikos, 'house') + vĺŒμος (nomos, 'custom' or 'law'), hence 'rules of the house(hold)'. Current _____ models developed out of the broader field of political economy in the late 19th century, owing to a desire to use an empirical approach more akin to the physical sciences.
   a. Opportunity cost
   b. Economic
   c. Energy economics
   d. Inflation

6. In microeconomics, the _____ describes the minimum amount of money an individual needs to achieve some level of utility, given a utility function and prices.

   Formally, if there is a utility function u that describes preferences over L commodities, the _____

   $$e(p, u^*) : \mathbf{R}^L_+ \times \mathbf{R} \to \mathbf{R}$$

says what amount of money is needed to achieve a utility u* if prices are set by p. This function is defined by

$$e(p, u^*) = \min_{x \in \geq (u^*)} p \cdot x$$

where

$$\geq (u^*) = \{x \in \mathbf{R}^L_+ : u(x) \geq u^*\}$$

is the set of all packages that give utility at least as good as u*.

a. Indifference curve
b. Income elasticity of demand
c. Expenditure minimization problem
d. Expenditure function

7. _____ is a concept found in moral, political, and bioethical philosophy. Within these contexts, it refers to the capacity of a rational individual to make an informed, un-coerced decision. In moral and political philosophy, _____ is often used as the basis for determining moral responsibility for one's actions.

a. AD-IA Model
b. ACEA agreement
c. ACCRA Cost of Living Index
d. Autonomy

8. _____ is a common concept in economics, and gives rise to derived concepts such as consumer debt. Generally _____ is defined by opposition to production. But the precise definition can vary because different schools of economists define production quite differently.

a. Federal Reserve Bank Notes
b. Cash or share options
c. Foreclosure data providers
d. Consumption

9. In economics, the _____ is a single mathematical function used to express consumer spending. It was developed by John Maynard Keynes and detailed most famously in his book The General Theory of Employment, Interest, and Money. The function is used to calculate the amount of total consumption in an economy.

a. DAD-SAS model
b. Liquidity preference
c. Procyclical
d. Consumption function

10. In economics, the _____ is an empirical metric that quantifies induced consumption, the concept that the increase in personal consumer spending (consumption) that occurs with an increase in disposable income (income after taxes and transfers.) For example, if a household earns one extra dollar of disposable income, and the _____ is 0.65, then of that dollar, the household will spend 65 cents and save 35 cents.

Mathematically, the _____ (MPC) function is expressed as the derivative of the consumption (C) function with respect to disposable income (Y.)

a. Technology shock
b. Marginal propensity to import
c. Supply shock
d. Marginal propensity to consume

Chapter 10. Aggregate Expenditures

11. In economics, an _____ is any good or commodity, transported from one country to another country in a legitimate fashion, typically for use in trade. _____ goods or services are provided to foreign consumers by domestic producers. _____ is an important part of international trade.
    a. Export
    b. ACEA agreement
    c. AD-IA Model
    d. ACCRA Cost of Living Index

12. The _____ refers to the increase in saving (non-purchase of current goods and services) that results from an increase in income. For example, if a household earns one extra dollar, and the _____ is 0.35, then of that dollar, the household will spend 65 cents and save 35 cents. It can also go the other way, referring to the decrease in saving that results from a decrease in income.
    a. Solow residual
    b. Marginal propensity to save
    c. Real business cycle
    d. Robertson lag

13. In economics, the _____ or spending multiplier is the idea that an initial amount of spending (usually by the government) leads to increased consumption spending and so results in an increase in national income greater than the initial amount of spending. In other words, an initial change in aggregate demand causes a change in aggregate output for the economy that is a multiple of the initial change.

The existence of a _____ was initially proposed by Ralph George Hawtrey in 1931.

    a. Magical triangle
    b. Multiplier effect
    c. Keynesian cross
    d. Spending multiplier

14. An _____, in economics, is the amount by which the real Gross domestic product exceeds potential GDP. The real GDP is also known as GDP 'adjusted for inflation', 'constant prices' GDP or 'constant dollar' GDP, because it measures the aggregate output in a country's income accounts in a given year, expressed in base-year prices. On the other hand, the potential GDP is the quantity of real GDP when a country's economy is at full-employment.
    a. ACEA agreement
    b. ACCRA Cost of Living Index
    c. AD-IA Model
    d. Inflationary gap

15. The GDP gap or the _____ is the difference between potential GDP and actual GDP or actual output. The calculation for the _____ is Y-Y* where Y* is potential output and Y is actual output. If this calculation yields a positive number it is called an expansionary gap and indicates an economy in expansion; if the calculation yields a negative number it is called a recessionary gap and indicates an economy in recession.
    a. AD-IA Model
    b. ACEA agreement
    c. ACCRA Cost of Living Index
    d. Output gap

16. The GDP gap or the output gap is the difference between potential GDP and actual GDP or actual output. The calculation for the output gap is Y-Y* where Y* is potential output and Y is actual output. If this calculation yields a positive number it is called an expansionary gap and indicates an economy in expansion; if the calculation yields a negative number it is called a _____ and indicates an economy in recession.
    a. 130-30 fund
    b. 100-year flood
    c. Recessionary gap
    d. 1921 recession

17. To _____ is to impose a financial charge or other levy upon a taxpayer by a state or the functional equivalent of a state.

_____es are also imposed by many subnational entities. _____es consist of direct _____ or indirect _____, and may be paid in money or as its labour equivalent (often but not always unpaid.)

a. 100-year flood
b. 130-30 fund
c. 1921 recession
d. Tax

18. The term _____ refers to government debt, expenditures and revenues, or to finance (particularly financial revenue) in general.

- _____ deficit is the budget deficit of federal or local government
- _____ policy is the discretionary spending of governments. Contrasts with monetary policy.
- _____ year and _____ quarter are reporting periods for firms and other agencies.

a. Fiscal
b. Drawdown
c. Bucket shop
d. Procter ' Gamble

19. In economics, _____ is the use of government spending and revenue collection to influence the economy.

_____ can be contrasted with the other main type of economic policy, monetary policy, which attempts to stabilize the economy by controlling interest rates and the supply of money. The two main instruments of _____ are government spending and taxation.

a. Sustainable investment rule
b. 100-year flood
c. Fiscal policy
d. Fiscalism

20. The _____ is the multiplier principle in keynesian economics (formulated by John Maynard Keynes.) The multiplier is a rather simplistic version of this. It applies to any change in autonomous expenditure, in other words, a change in consumption, investment, government expenditure or net exports.

a. Liquidity trap
b. Complex multiplier
c. Natural rate of unemployment
d. Microfoundations

21. The _____ is the apparent contradiction that although water is on the whole more useful, in terms of survival, than diamonds, diamonds command a higher price in the market. The economist Adam Smith is often considered to be the classic presenter of this paradox. Nicolaus Copernicus, John Locke, John Law and others had previously tried to explain the disparity.

a. Paradox of value
b. 130-30 fund
c. St. Petersburg paradox
d. 100-year flood

22. The _____ is a paradox of economics propounded by John Maynard Keynes. The paradox states that if everyone saves more money during times of recession, then aggregate demand will fall and will in turn lower total savings in the population because of the decrease in consumption and economic growth.

Chapter 10. Aggregate Expenditures

The argument is that, in equilibrium, total income (and thus demand) must equal total output, and that total investment must equal total saving.

a. Keynesian cross
c. Paradox of thrift

b. Spending multiplier
d. Speculative demand

23. A _____ association is a financial institution that specializes in accepting savings deposits and making mortgage and other loans. The S'L or thrift term is mainly used in the United States; similar institutions in the United Kingdom, Ireland and some Commonwealth countries include building societies and trustee savings banks.

They are often mutually held, meaning that the depositors and borrowers are members with voting rights, and have the ability to direct the financial and managerial goals of the organization, similar to the policyholders of a mutual insurance company.

a. Collective investment scheme
c. Fonds commun de placement

b. Participating policy
d. Savings and Loan

24. In economics, _____ is the total demand for final goods and services in the economy (Y) at a given time and price level. It is the amount of goods and services in the economy that will be purchased at all possible price levels. This is the demand for the gross domestic product of a country when inventory levels are static.

a. Aggregate expenditure
c. Aggregate supply

b. Aggregation problem
d. Aggregate demand

25. In economics, _____ is the total supply of goods and services produced by a national economy during a specific time period. It is the total amount of goods and services in the economy available at all possible price levels.

a. Aggregate demand
c. Aggregate expenditure

b. Aggregate supply
d. Aggregation problem

26. Economics:

- _____ ,the desire to own something and the ability to pay for it
- _____ curve,a graphic representation of a _____ schedule
- _____ deposit, the money in checking accounts
- _____ pull theory,the theory that inflation occurs when _____ for goods and services exceeds existing supplies
- _____ schedule,a table that lists the quantity of a good a person will buy it each different price
- _____ side economics,the school of economics at believes government spending and tax cuts open economy by raising _____

a. Demand
c. McKesson ' Robbins scandal

b. Production
d. Variability

27. In statistics, a _____ is a mathematical relationship in which two occurrences have no causal connection, yet it may be inferred that they do, due to a certain third, unseen factor (referred to as a 'confounding factor' or 'lurking variable'.) The _____ gives an impression of a worthy link between two groups that is invalid when objectively examined.

The misleading correlation between two variables is produced through the operation of a third causal variable.

- a. 130-30 fund
- b. Spurious relationship
- c. 1921 recession
- d. 100-year flood

28. The _____ was an act signed into law on June 17, 1930, that raised U.S. tariffs on over 20,000 imported goods to record levels. In the United States 1,028 economists signed a petition against this legislation, and after it was passed, many countries retaliated with their own increased tariffs on U.S. goods, and American exports and imports were reduced by more than half.

Although rated capacity had increased tremendously, actual output, income, and expenditure had not.

- a. Patent Law Treaty
- b. Loss of use
- c. Smoot-Hawley Tariff Act
- d. Judgment summons

29. _____ was an American economist, statistician and public intellectual, and a recipient of the Nobel Memorial Prize in Economic Sciences. He is best known among scholars for his theoretical and empirical research, especially consumption analysis, monetary history and theory, and for his demonstration of the complexity of stabilization policy. A global public followed his restatement of a political philosophy that insisted on minimizing the role of government in favor of the private sector.

- a. Milton Friedman
- b. Adolph Fischer
- c. Adam Smith
- d. Adolf Hitler

Chapter 11. Fiscal Policy in Action

1. In economics, a _____ is a redistribution of income in the market system. These payments are considered to be nonexhaustive because they do not directly absorb resources or create output. Examples of certain _____s include welfare (financial aid), social security, and government subsidies for certain businesses (firms.)
   a. 100-year flood
   b. 130-30 fund
   c. Transfer payment
   d. 1921 recession

2. A _____ is the transfer of wealth from one party (such as a person or company) to another. A _____ is usually made in exchange for the provision of goods, services or both, or to fulfill a legal obligation.

   The simplest and oldest form of _____ is barter, the exchange of one good or service for another.

   a. Soft count
   b. Social gravity
   c. Payment
   d. Going concern

3. To _____ is to impose a financial charge or other levy upon a taxpayer by a state or the functional equivalent of a state.

   _____es are also imposed by many subnational entities. _____es consist of direct _____ or indirect _____, and may be paid in money or as its labour equivalent (often but not always unpaid.)

   a. 100-year flood
   b. 130-30 fund
   c. Tax
   d. 1921 recession

4. The _____ or gross domestic income (GDI), a basic measure of an economy's economic performance, is the market value of all final goods and services produced within the borders of a nation in a year. _____ can be defined in three ways, all of which are conceptually identical. First, it is equal to the total expenditures for all final goods and services produced within the country in a stipulated period of time (usually a 365-day year.)
   a. Market structure
   b. Monopolistic competition
   c. Countercyclical
   d. Gross domestic product

5. An _____ is a tax levied on the financial income of people, corporations, or other legal entities. Various _____ systems exist, with varying degrees of tax incidence. Income taxation can be progressive, proportional, or regressive.
   a. ACCRA Cost of Living Index
   b. AD-IA Model
   c. ACEA agreement
   d. Income tax

6. Total _____ is defined by the United States' Bureau of Economic Analysis as

   income received by persons from all sources. It includes income received from participation in production as well as from government and business transfer payments. It is the sum of compensation of employees (received), supplements to wages and salaries, proprietors' income with inventory valuation adjustment (IVA) and capital consumption adjustment (CCAdj), rental income of persons with CCAdj, _____ receipts on assets, and personal current transfer receipts, less contributions for government social insurance.

   a. Personal income
   b. Dividend Discount Model
   c. Bidding
   d. Greater fool theory

7. _____ is a common concept in economics, and gives rise to derived concepts such as consumer debt. Generally _____ is defined by opposition to production. But the precise definition can vary because different schools of economists define production quite differently.

- a. Consumption
- b. Federal Reserve Bank Notes
- c. Foreclosure data providers
- d. Cash or share options

8. In a company, _____ is the sum of all financial records of salaries, wages, bonuses and deductions.

A paycheck, is traditionally a paper document issued by an employer to pay an employee for services rendered. While most commonly used in the United States, recently the physical paycheck has been increasingly replaced by electronic direct deposit to bank accounts.

- a. 100-year flood
- b. Total Expense Ratio
- c. Tax expense
- d. Payroll

9. _____ refers to a tax levied by various jurisdictions on the profits made by companies or associations. It is a tax on the value of the corporation's profits.

The measure of taxable profits varies from country to country.

- a. Captive unit
- b. Business process reengineering
- c. Business engineering
- d. Corporate tax

10. In economics, _____ is the analysis of the effect of a particular tax on the distribution of economic welfare. _____ is said to 'fall' upon the group that, at the end of the day, bears the burden of the tax. The key concept is that the _____ or tax burden does not depend on where the revenue is collected, but on the price elasticity of demand and price elasticity of supply.

- a. 130-30 fund
- b. 1921 recession
- c. 100-year flood
- d. Tax incidence

11. _____ is the concept or idea of fairness in economics, particularly as to taxation or welfare economics.

In welfare economics, _____ may be distinguished from economic efficiency in overall evaluation of social welfare. Although '_____' has broader uses, it may be posed as a counterpart to economic inequality in yielding a 'good' distribution of welfare.

- a. AD-IA Model
- b. ACCRA Cost of Living Index
- c. Equity
- d. ACEA agreement

12. Under the system of feudalism, a _____, fief, feud, feoff often consisted of inheritable lands or revenue-producing property granted by a liege lord, generally to a vassal, in return for a form of allegiance, originally to give him the means to fulfill his military duties when called upon. However anything of value could be held in fief, such as an office, a right of exploitation (e.g., hunting, fishing) or any other type of revenue, rather than the land it comes from.

Originally, the feudal institution of vassalage did not imply the giving or receiving of landholdings (which were granted only as a reward for loyalty), but by the eighth century the giving of a landholding was becoming standard.

a. 1921 recession
b. 130-30 fund
c. Fiefdom
d. 100-year flood

13. _____s is the social science that studies the production, distribution, and consumption of goods and services. The term _____s comes from the Ancient Greek oá¼°κονομῖα from oá¼¶κος (oikos, 'house') + vῐΌεμος (nomos, 'custom' or 'law'), hence 'rules of the house(hold)'. Current _____ models developed out of the broader field of political economy in the late 19th century, owing to a desire to use an empirical approach more akin to the physical sciences.

a. Inflation
b. Opportunity cost
c. Energy economics
d. Economic

14. _____ is used to refer to a number of related concepts. It is the using resources in such a way as to maximize the production of goods and services. A system can be called economically efficient if:

- No one can be made better off without making someone else worse off.
- More output cannot be obtained without increasing the amount of inputs.
- Production proceeds at the lowest possible per-unit cost.

These definitions of efficiency are not equivalent, but they are all encompassed by the idea that nothing more can be achieved given the resources available.

An economic system is more efficient if it can provide more goods and services for society without using more resources.

a. Efficient contract theory
b. ACEA agreement
c. Economic efficiency
d. ACCRA Cost of Living Index

15. A _____ is a tax system with a constant tax rate. Usually the term _____ would refer to household income (and sometimes corporate profits) being taxed at one marginal rate, in contrast with progressive taxes that may vary according to such parameters as income or usage levels. _____es generally offer simplicity in the tax code, which has been reported to increase compliance and decrease administration costs.

a. Flat tax
b. 1921 recession
c. 100-year flood
d. 130-30 fund

16. A _____ is a tax by which the tax rate increases as the taxable amount increases. 'Progressive' describes a distribution effect on income or expenditure, referring to the way the rate progresses from low to high, where the average tax rate is less than the marginal tax rate. It can be applied to individual taxes or to a tax system as a whole; a year, multi-year, or lifetime.

a. Proportional tax
b. 130-30 fund
c. 100-year flood
d. Progressive tax

17. A _____ is a tax imposed so that the tax rate is fixed as the amount subject to taxation increases. In simple terms, it imposes an equal burden (relative to resources) on the rich and poor. 'Proportional' describes a distribution effect on income or expenditure, referring to the way the rate remains consistent (does not progress from 'low to high' or 'high to low' as income or consumption changes), where the marginal tax rate is equal to the average tax rate.

   a. 130-30 fund   b. 100-year flood

   c. Regressive tax   d. Proportional tax

18. A _____ is a tax imposed in such a manner that the tax rate decreases as the amount subject to taxation increases. In simple terms, a _____ imposes a greater burden (relative to resources) on the poor than on the rich -- there is an inverse relationship between the tax rate and the taxpayer's ability to pay as measured by assets, consumption, or income. 'Regressive' describes a distribution effect on income or expenditure, referring to the way the rate progresses from high to low, where the average tax rate exceeds the marginal tax rate.

   a. Regressive tax   b. 100-year flood

   c. Proportional tax   d. 130-30 fund

19. A poll tax, _____ fixed amount per individual in accordance with the census (as opposed to a percentage of income.) When a corvée is commuted for cash payment, in effect it becomes a poll tax (and vice versa, if a poll tax obligation can be worked off.) Poll taxes were important sources of revenue for many governments from ancient times until the 19th century.

   a. Privatized tax collection   b. Tax Executives Institute

   c. Cess   d. Head tax

20. The _____ is the means by which the federal government of the United States accounts for excess paid-in contributions from workers and employers to the Social Security system that are not required to fund current benefit payments to retirees, survivors, and the disabled or to pay administrative expenses. More importantly, the trust fund also contains the securities that will be redeemed to make benefit payments in the future when contributions derived from payroll taxes and self-employment contributions no longer are sufficient to fully fund then-current benefit payments. (The controversy over its meaningfulness is a topic of the sustainability of the unified Federal budget.)

   a. Retirement Insurance Benefits   b. Legacy debt

   c. Social Security trust fund   d. Social Security Disability Insurance

21. In economics, _____ is the transfer of income, wealth or property from some individuals to others.

One premise of _____ is that money should be distributed to benefit the poorer members of society, and that the rich have an obligation to assist the poor, thus creating a more financially egalitarian society. Another argument is that the rich exploit the poor or otherwise gain unfair benefits.

   a. Redistribution   b. 130-30 fund

   c. 100-year flood   d. 1921 recession

22. A _____ is a fraudulent investment operation that pays returns to investors from their own money or money paid by subsequent investors rather than from any actual profit earned. The _____ usually offers returns that other investments cannot guarantee in order to entice new investors, in the form of short-term returns that are either abnormally high or unusually consistent. The perpetuation of the returns that a _____ advertises and pays requires an ever-increasing flow of money from investors in order to keep the scheme going.

Chapter 11. Fiscal Policy in Action

a. Ponzi scheme
b. Reloading scam
c. Hustling
d. Bogus escrow

23. An _____ is a retirement plan account that provides some tax advantages for retirement savings in the United States.

There are a number of different types of _____s, which may be either employer-provided or self-provided plans. The types include:

- Roth _____ - contributions are made with after-tax assets, all transactions within the _____ have no tax impact, and withdrawals are usually tax-free. Named for Senator William Roth.
- Traditional _____ - contributions are often tax-deductible (often simplified as 'money is deposited before tax' or 'contributions are made with pre-tax assets'), all transactions and earnings within the _____ have no tax impact, and withdrawals at retirement are taxed as income (except for those portions of the withdrawal corresponding to contributions that were not deducted.) Depending upon the nature of the contribution, a traditional _____ may be referred to as a 'deductible _____' or a 'non-deductible _____.'
- SEP _____ - a provision that allows an employer (typically a small business or self-employed individual) to make retirement plan contributions into a Traditional _____ established in the employee's name, instead of to a pension fund account in the company's name.
- SIMPLE _____ - a simplified employee pension plan that allows both employer and employee contributions, similar to a 401(k) plan, but with lower contribution limits and simpler (and thus less costly) administration. Although it is termed an _____, it is treated separately.
- Self-Directed _____ - a self-directed _____ that permits the account holder to make investments on behalf of the retirement plan.

There are two other subtypes of _____, named Rollover _____ and Conduit _____, that are viewed as obsolete under current tax law (their functions have been subsumed by the Traditional _____) by some; but this tax law is set to expire unless extended. However, some individuals still maintain these accounts in order to keep track of the source of these assets.

a. ACCRA Cost of Living Index
b. ACEA agreement
c. AD-IA Model
d. Individual Retirement Arrangement

24. _____ is the point where a person stops employment completely. A person may also semi-retire and keep some sort of _____ job, out of choice rather than necessity. This usually happens upon reaching a determined age, when physical conditions don't allow the person to work any more (by illness or accident), or even for personal choice (usually in the presence of an adequate pension or personal savings.)

a. Termination of employment
b. 100-year flood
c. Layoff
d. Retirement

25. _____ is the process of changing the way taxes are collected or managed by the government.

_____ers have different goals. Some seek to reduce the level of taxation of all people by the government.

a. Nil-rate band
c. Special-purpose local-option sales tax
b. Tax break
d. Tax reform

26. To tax is to impose a financial charge or other levy upon a taxpayer by a state or the functional equivalent of a state.

_____ are also imposed by many subnational entities. _____ consist of direct tax or indirect tax, and may be paid in money or as its labour equivalent (often but not always unpaid.)

a. 130-30 fund
c. 1921 recession
b. 100-year flood
d. Taxes

27. A _____ is a tax on spending on goods and services. The term refers to a system with a tax base of consumption. It usually takes the form of an indirect tax, such as a sales tax or value added tax.

a. 1921 recession
c. 100-year flood
b. 130-30 fund
d. Consumption tax

28. _____ is the a method of technical and economic research of the systems for purpose to optimize a parity between system's consumer functions or properties and expenses to achieve those functions or properties.

This methodology for continuous perfection of production, industrial technologies, organizational structures was developed by Juryj Sobolev in 1948 at the 'Perm telephone factory'

- 1948 Juryj Sobolev - the first success in application of a method analysis at the 'Perm telephone factory' .
- 1949 - the first application for the invention as result of use of the new method.

Today in economically developed countries practically each enterprise or the company use methodology of the kind of functional-cost analysis as a practice of the quality management, most full satisfying to principles of standards of series ISO 9000.

- Interest of consumer not in products itself, but the advantage which it will receive from its usage.
- The consumer aspires to reduce his expenses
- Functions needed by consumer can be executed in the various ways, and, hence, with various efficiency and expenses. Among possible alternatives of realization of functions exist such in which the parity of quality and the price is the optimal for the consumer.

The goal of _____ is achievement of the highest consumer satisfaction of production at simultaneous decrease in all kinds of industrial expenses Classical _____ has three English synonyms - Value Engineering, Value Management, Value Analysis.

a. Staple financing
c. Willingness to pay
b. Function cost analysis
d. Monopoly wage

Chapter 11. Fiscal Policy in Action

29. _____ refers to the additional value of a commodity over the cost of commodities used to produce it from the previous stage of production. An example is the price of gasoline at the pump over the price of the oil in it. In national accounts used in macroeconomics, it refers to the contribution of the factors of production, i.e., land, labor, and capital goods, to raising the value of a product and corresponds to the incomes received by the owners of these factors.

   a. Solow residual
   b. Value added
   c. Full employment
   d. Hodrick-Prescott filter

30. _____ , or goods and services tax (GST) is a consumption tax levied on value added. In contrast to sales tax, _____ is neutral with respect to the number of passages that there are between the producer and the final consumer; where sales tax is levied on total value at each stage, the result is a cascade (downstream taxes levied on upstream taxes.) A _____ is an indirect tax, in that the tax is collected from someone who does not bear the entire cost of the tax.

   a. 1921 recession
   b. 100-year flood
   c. Value added tax
   d. 130-30 fund

31. _____ are the income that is gained by governments because of taxation of the people.

Just as there are different types of tax, the form in which _____ is collected also differs; furthermore, the agency that collects the tax may not be part of central government, but may be an alternative third-party licenced to collect tax which they themselves will use. For example:

- In the UK, the DVLA collects road tax, which is then passed on the treasury.

_____s on purchases can come from two forms: 'tax' itself is a percentage of the price added to the purchase (such as sales tax in US states, or VAT in the UK), while 'duty' is a fixed amount added to the purchase price (such as is commonly found on cigarettes.) In order to calculate the total tax raised from these sales, we must work out the effective tax rate multiplied by the quantity supplied.

   a. Tax revenue
   b. Taxable wage
   c. Tax and spend
   d. Taxation as slavery

32. _____ is a policy or ideology of violence intended to intimidate or cause terror for the purpose of 'exerting pressure on decision making by state bodies.' The term 'terror' is largely used to indicate clandestine, low-intensity violence that targets civilians and generates public fear. Thus 'terror' is distinct from asymmetric warfare, and violates the concept of a common law of war in which civilian life is regarded. The term '-ism' is used to indicate an ideology --typically one that claims its attacks are in the domain of a 'just war' concept, though most condemn such as crimes against humanity.

   a. 100-year flood
   b. 1921 recession
   c. Terrorism
   d. 130-30 fund

Chapter 12. Economic Growth

1. _____s is the social science that studies the production, distribution, and consumption of goods and services. The term _____s comes from the Ancient Greek oá¼°κονομῖα from oá¼¶κος (oikos, 'house') + vĺŒµος (nomos, 'custom' or 'law'), hence 'rules of the house(hold)'. Current _____ models developed out of the broader field of political economy in the late 19th century, owing to a desire to use an empirical approach more akin to the physical sciences.
   a. Opportunity cost
   b. Inflation
   c. Energy economics
   d. Economic

2. _____ is the increase in the amount of the goods and services produced by an economy over time. It is conventionally measured as the percent rate of increase in real gross domestic product, or real GDP. Growth is usually calculated in real terms, i.e. inflation-adjusted terms, in order to net out the effect of inflation on the price of the goods and services produced.
   a. ACCRA Cost of Living Index
   b. AD-IA Model
   c. ACEA agreement
   d. Economic growth

3. The _____ or gross domestic income (GDI), a basic measure of an economy's economic performance, is the market value of all final goods and services produced within the borders of a nation in a year. _____ can be defined in three ways, all of which are conceptually identical. First, it is equal to the total expenditures for all final goods and services produced within the country in a stipulated period of time (usually a 365-day year.)
   a. Monopolistic competition
   b. Market structure
   c. Countercyclical
   d. Gross domestic product

4. _____ in economics refers to metrics and measures of output from production processes, per unit of input. Labor _____, for example, is typically measured as a ratio of output per labor-hour, an input. _____ may be conceived of as a metrics of the technical or engineering efficiency of production.
   a. Production-possibility frontier
   b. Productivity
   c. Piece work
   d. Fordism

5. _____ is a term used in national accounts statistics and macroeconomics. It basically refers to the net additions to the (physical) capital stock in an accounting period, or, to the value of the increase of the capital stock; though it may occasionally also refer to the (growth of the) total stock of capital formed.

   Thus, in UNSNA, _____ equals fixed capital investment, the increase in the value of inventories held, plus (net) lending to foreign countries, during an accounting period.

   a. Capital flight
   b. Consumption of fixed capital
   c. Capital intensity
   d. Capital formation

6. _____ can be generally defined as the course of action or inaction taken by governmental entities with regard to a particular issue or set of issues. Other scholars define it as a system of 'courses of action, regulatory measures, laws, and funding priorities concerning a given topic promulgated by a governmental entity or its representatives.' _____ is commonly embodied 'in constitutions, legislative acts, and judicial decisions.'

   In the United States, this concept refers not only to the end result of policies, but more broadly to the decision-making and analysis of governmental decisions. _____ is also considered an academic discipline, as it is studied by professors and students at _____ schools of major universities throughout the country.

Chapter 12. Economic Growth

    a. 130-30 fund
    b. 1921 recession
    c. 100-year flood
    d. Public policy

7. _____ is a fee paid on borrowed assets. It is the price paid for the use of borrowed money , or, money earned by deposited funds . Assets that are sometimes lent with _____ include money, shares, consumer goods through hire purchase, major assets such as aircraft, and even entire factories in finance lease arrangements.

    a. Asset protection
    b. Internal debt
    c. Insolvency
    d. Interest

8. An _____ is the price a borrower pays for the use of money they do not own, for instance a small company might borrow from a bank to kick start their business, and the return a lender receives for deferring the use of funds, by lending it to the borrower. _____s are normally expressed as a percentage rate over the period of one year.

_____s targets are also a vital tool of monetary policy and are used to control variables like investment, inflation, and unemployment.

    a. Arrow-Debreu model
    b. Enterprise value
    c. ACCRA Cost of Living Index
    d. Interest rate

9. The _____ is the weighted-average most likely outcome in gambling, probability theory, economics or finance.

What Does _____ Mean? The average of a probability distribution of possible returns, calculated by using the following formula:

E(R)= Sum: probability (in scenario i) * the return (in scenario i)

How do you calculate the average of a probability distribution? As denoted by the above formula, simply take the probability of each possible return outcome and multiply it by the return outcome itself. For example, if you knew a given investment had a 50% chance of earning a 10% return, a 25% chance of earning 20% and a 25% chance of earning -10%, the _____ would be equal to 7.5%:

= (0.5) (0.1) + (0.25) (0.2) + (0.25) (-0.1) = 0.075 = 7.5%

Although this is what you expect the return to be, there is no guarantee that it will be the actual return.

    a. ACEA agreement
    b. ACCRA Cost of Living Index
    c. AD-IA Model
    d. Expected return

10. In economics and sociology, an _____ is any factor (financial or non-financial) that enables or motivates a particular course of action, or counts as a reason for preferring one choice to the alternatives. It is an expectation that encourages people to behave in a certain way. Since human beings are purposeful creatures, the study of _____ structures is central to the study of all economic activity (both in terms of individual decision-making and in terms of co-operation and competition within a larger institutional structure.)

a. Incentive
b. Isocost
c. Epstein-Zin preferences
d. Economic reform

11. A _____ is a tax charged on capital gains, the profit realized on the sale of a non-inventory asset that was purchased at a lower price. The most common capital gains are realized from the sale of stocks, bonds, precious metals and property. Not all countries implement a _____ and most have different rates of taxation for individuals and corporations.
a. Capital gains tax
b. Tax resistance
c. Potentially dangerous taxpayer
d. Tax deferral

12. To _____ is to impose a financial charge or other levy upon a taxpayer by a state or the functional equivalent of a state.

_____es are also imposed by many subnational entities. _____es consist of direct _____ or indirect _____, and may be paid in money or as its labour equivalent (often but not always unpaid.)

a. 130-30 fund
b. 1921 recession
c. 100-year flood
d. Tax

13. In economics, an externality or spillover of an economic transaction is an impact on a party that is not directly involved in the transaction. In such a case, prices do not reflect the full costs or benefits in production or consumption of a product or service. A positive impact is called an _____, while a negative impact is called an external cost.
a. AD-IA Model
b. External benefit
c. ACEA agreement
d. ACCRA Cost of Living Index

14. A _____ is the exclusive authority to determine how a resource is used, whether that resource is owned by government or by individuals. All economic goods have a _____s attribute. This attribute has three broad components

1. The right to use the good
2. The right to earn income from the good
3. The right to transfer the good to others

The concept of _____s as used by economists and legal scholars are related but distinct. The distinction is largely seen in the economists' focus on the ability of an individual or collective to control the use of the good.

a. Holder in due course
b. Property right
c. Post-sale restraint
d. High-reeve

15. The phrase _____, according to the Organization for Economic Co-operation and Development, refers to 'creative work undertaken on a systematic basis in order to increase the stock of knowledge, including knowledge of man, culture and society, and the use of this stock of knowledge to devise new applications [sic]'

New product design and development is more than often a crucial factor in the survival of a company. In an industry that is fast changing, firms must continually revise their design and range of products. This is necessary due to continuous technology change and development as well as other competitors and the changing preference of customers.

a. Research and development
b. 1921 recession
c. 100-year flood
d. 130-30 fund

16. In economics, a _____ exists when a specific individual or enterprise has sufficient control over a particular product or service to determine significantly the terms on which other individuals shall have access to it. Monopolies are thus characterized by a lack of economic competition for the good or service that they provide and a lack of viable substitute goods. The verb 'monopolize' refers to the process by which a firm gains persistently greater market share than what is expected under perfect competition.

a. 1921 recession
b. 100-year flood
c. 130-30 fund
d. Monopoly

17. In economics, endogenous growth theory or _____ was developed in the 1980s as a response to criticism of the neo-classical growth model.

In neo-classical growth models, the long-run rate of growth is exogenously determined by either assuming a savings rate (the Harrod-Domar model) or a rate of technical progress (Solow model.) However, the savings rate and rate of technological progress remain unexplained.

a. Real prices and ideal prices
b. Kondratiev waves
c. Cobweb model
d. New growth theory

18. The _____ is a heterodox school of economics that emphasizes the spontaneous organizing power of the price mechanism. It holds that the complexity of subjective human choices makes mathematical modelling of the evolving market extremely difficult and advocates a laissez faire approach to the economy. _____ economists advocate the enforcement of voluntary contractual agreements between economic agents, but otherwise the smallest imposition of coercive force on commercial transactions.

a. ACEA agreement
b. Economic calculation problem
c. ACCRA Cost of Living Index
d. Austrian school

19. _____ is a school of macroeconomic thought that argues that economic growth can be most effectively created using incentives for people to produce (supply) goods and services, such as adjusting income tax and capital gains tax rates, and by allowing greater flexibility by reducing regulation. Consumers will then benefit from a greater supply of goods and services at lower prices.

The term _____ was coined by journalist Jude Wanniski in 1975, and popularized the ideas of economists Robert Mundell and Arthur Laffer.

a. Commodity trading advisors
b. Clap note
c. Supply-side economics
d. Fiscal stimulus plans

20. In economics, the _____ is used to illustrate the idea that increases in the rate of taxation do not necessarily increase tax revenue. (For instance, whereas a 0% income tax rate will generate no revenue, neither will a 100% rate, as citizens will have no incentive to make money.) Increasing taxes beyond the peak of the curve point will decrease tax revenue.

a. 100-year flood
b. 1921 recession
c. 130-30 fund
d. Laffer curve

Chapter 13. Money, Banking, and the Federal Reserve

1. Bartering is a medium in which goods or services are directly exchanged for other goods and/or services, without the use of money. It can be bilateral or multilateral, and usually exists parallel to monetary systems in most developed countries, though to a very limited extent. _____ usually replaces money as the method of exchange in times of monetary crisis, when the currency is unstable and devalued by hyperinflation.
   a. Community-based economics
   b. Meitheal
   c. New Economics Foundation
   d. Barter

2. A _____ is something for which there is demand, but which is supplied without qualitative differentiation across a market. It is a product that is the same no matter who produces it, such as petroleum, notebook paper, or milk. In other words, copper is copper.
   a. 100-year flood
   b. Soft commodity
   c. Hard commodity
   d. Commodity

3. _____ is money whose value comes from a commodity out of which it is made. It is objects that have value in themselves as well as for use as money.

   Examples of commodities that have been used as mediums of exchange include gold, silver, copper, salt, peppercorns, large stones, decorated belts, shells, alcohol, cigarettes, cannabis, candy, barley etc.

   a. Commodity money
   b. Fiat money
   c. Reserve currency
   d. Currency competition

4. The _____ is the central banking system of the United States. Created in 1913 by the enactment of the Federal Reserve Act (signed by Woodrow Wilson), it is a quasi-public and quasi-private (government entity with private components) banking system that comprises (1) the presidentially appointed Board of Governors of the _____ in Washington, D.C.; (2) the Federal Open Market Committee; (3) twelve regional Federal Reserve Banks located in major cities throughout the nation acting as fiscal agents for the U.S. Treasury, each with its own nine-member board of directors; (4) numerous other private U.S. member banks, which subscribe to required amounts of non-transferable stock in their regional Federal Reserve Banks; and (5) various advisory councils. Since February 2006, Ben Bernanke has served as the Chairman of the Board of Governors of the _____.
   a. Term auction facility
   b. Federal Reserve System
   c. Monetary Policy Report to the Congress
   d. Federal Reserve System Open Market Account

5. _____ is money declared by a government to be legal tender. The term derives from the Latin fiat, meaning 'let it be done'. _____ achieves value because a government accepts it in payment of taxes and says it can be used within the country as a 'tender' to pay all debts.
   a. Devaluation
   b. Fiat money
   c. World currency
   d. Currency board

Chapter 13. Money, Banking, and the Federal Reserve

6. _____ has several particular meanings:

   - in mathematics
     - _____ function
     - Euler _____
     - _____
     - _____ subgroup
     - method of _____s (partial differential equations)
   - in physics and engineering
     - any _____ curve that shows the relationship between certain input- and output parameters, e.g.
     - an I-V or current-voltage _____ is the current in a circuit as a function of the applied voltage
     - Receiver-Operator _____
   - in fiction
     - in Dungeons ' Dragons, _____ is another name for ability score

   a. Demand
   b. Russian financial crisis
   c. Technocracy
   d. Characteristic

7. A _____ is an intermediary used in trade to avoid the inconveniences of a pure barter system.

By contrast, as William Stanley Jevons argued, in a barter system there must be a coincidence of wants before two people can trade - one must want exactly what the other has to offer, when and where it is offered, so that the exchange can occur. A _____ permits the value of goods to be assessed and rendered in terms of the intermediary, most often, a form of money widely accepted to buy any other good.

   a. Labour economics
   b. Consumer theory
   c. Price revolution
   d. Medium of exchange

8. To act as a _____, a commodity, a form of money stored, and retrieved - and be predictably useful when it is so retrieved.

This is distinct from the standard of deferred payment function which requires acceptability to parties one owes a debt to and a minimum of opportunity to cheat others.

   a. Petrodollar
   b. Fiat money
   c. Store of value
   d. World currency

9. A _____ is a standard monetary unit of measurement of the market value/cost of goods, services, or assets. It is one of three well-known functions of money. It lends meaning to profits, losses, liability, or assets.
   a. ACEA agreement
   b. ACCRA Cost of Living Index
   c. AD-IA Model
   d. Unit of account

10. _____ is the a method of technical and economic research of the systems for purpose to optimize a parity between system's consumer functions or properties and expenses to achieve those functions or properties.

Chapter 13. Money, Banking, and the Federal Reserve

This methodology for continuous perfection of production, industrial technologies, organizational structures was developed by Juryj Sobolev in 1948 at the 'Perm telephone factory'

- 1948 Juryj Sobolev - the first success in application of a method analysis at the 'Perm telephone factory' .
- 1949 - the first application for the invention as result of use of the new method.

Today in economically developed countries practically each enterprise or the company use methodology of the kind of functional-cost analysis as a practice of the quality management, most full satisfying to principles of standards of series ISO 9000.

- Interest of consumer not in products itself, but the advantage which it will receive from its usage.
- The consumer aspires to reduce his expenses
- Functions needed by consumer can be executed in the various ways, and, hence, with various efficiency and expenses. Among possible alternatives of realization of functions exist such in which the parity of quality and the price is the optimal for the consumer.

The goal of _____ is achievement of the highest consumer satisfaction of production at simultaneous decrease in all kinds of industrial expenses Classical _____ has three English synonyms - Value Engineering, Value Management, Value Analysis.

a. Staple financing
c. Willingness to pay
b. Monopoly wage
d. Function cost analysis

11. Economics:

- _____, the desire to own something and the ability to pay for it
- _____ curve, a graphic representation of a _____ schedule
- _____ deposit, the money in checking accounts
- _____ pull theory, the theory that inflation occurs when _____ for goods and services exceeds existing supplies
- _____ schedule, a table that lists the quantity of a good a person will buy it each different price
- _____ side economics, the school of economics at believes government spending and tax cuts open economy by raising _____

a. McKesson ' Robbins scandal
c. Variability
b. Production
d. Demand

12. _____ is a type of bank account where the money in the account is legally able to be withdrawn immediately upon demand (or 'at call'.) This type of bank account can also be referred to as a 'cheque' or 'checking' or transactional account.

This type of bank account, allowing immediate conversion of the account balance into cash or withdrawal to another account, can be contrasted with a time deposit (also known as a certificate of deposit or term deposit), where the funds are not legally available for immediate withdrawal by the depositor.

Chapter 13. Money, Banking, and the Federal Reserve

a. Debt rescheduling
b. Tangible Common Equity
c. Clawbacks in economic development
d. Demand deposit

13. Market _____ is a business, economics or investment term that refers to an asset's ability to be easily converted through an act of buying or selling without causing a significant movement in the price and with minimum loss of value. Money, or cash on hand, is the most liquid asset. An act of exchange of a less liquid asset with a more liquid asset is called liquidation.
   a. 100-year flood
   b. 130-30 fund
   c. Liquidity
   d. 1921 recession

14. _____ is the net revenue derived from the issuing of currency.

_____ derived from specie - metal coins - arises from the difference between the face value of a coin and the cost of producing, distributing and retiring it from circulation.

_____ derived from notes is more indirect, being the difference between interest earned on securities acquired in exchange for bank notes and the costs of producing and distributing those notes.

   a. Seigniorage
   b. Money Tracker
   c. 100-year flood
   d. 130-30 fund

15. A _____ is a money deposit at a banking institution that cannot be withdrawn for a certain 'term' or period of time. When the term is over it can be withdrawn or it can be held for another term. Generally speaking, the longer the term the better the yield on the money.
   a. Deposit market share
   b. Finance charge
   c. Fractional-reserve banking
   d. Time deposit

16. In financial accounting, a _____ or statement of financial position is a summary of a person's or organization's balances. Assets, liabilities and ownership equity are listed as of a specific date, such as the end of its financial year. A _____ is often described as a snapshot of a company's financial condition.
   a. 100-year flood
   b. Balance sheet
   c. 130-30 fund
   d. 1921 recession

17. _____ are banks' holdings of deposits in accounts with their central bank (for instance the European Central Bank or the Federal Reserve, in the latter case including federal funds), plus currency that is physically held in bank vaults (vault cash.) The central banks of some nations set minimum reserve requirements. Even when no requirements are set, banks commonly wish to hold some reserves, called desired reserves, against unexpected events.
   a. Sweep account
   b. Structuring
   c. Bilateral netting
   d. Bank reserves

18. The _____ established the Federal Deposit Insurance Corporation (FDIC) in the United States and included banking reforms, some of which were designed to control speculation. Some provisions such as Regulation Q, which allowed the Federal Reserve to regulate interest rates in savings accounts, were repealed by the Depository Institutions Deregulation and Monetary Control Act of 1980. Provisions that prohibit a bank holding company from owning other financial companies were repealed on November 12, 1999, by the Gramm-Leach-Bliley Act.

a. 100-year flood
b. 130-30 fund
c. 1921 recession
d. Glass-Steagall Act of 1933

19. In finance, a _____ is a debt security, in which the authorized issuer owes the holders a debt and, depending on the terms of the _____, is obliged to pay interest (the coupon) and/or to repay the principal at a later date, termed maturity. A _____ is a formal contract to repay borrowed money with interest at fixed intervals.

Thus a _____ is like a loan: the issuer is the borrower (debtor), the holder is the lender (creditor), and the coupon is the interest.

a. Prize Bond
b. Zero-coupon
c. Callable
d. Bond

20. The _____ consists of a number of economic theories which describe the nature of the firm, company including its existence, its behaviour, and its relationship with the market.

In simplified terms, the _____ aims to answer these questions:

1. Existence - why do firms emerge, why are not all transactions in the economy mediated over the market?
2. Boundaries - why the boundary between firms and the market is located exactly there? Which transactions are performed internally and which are negotiated on the market?
3. Organization - why are firms structured in such specific way? What is the interplay of formal and informal relationships?

Despite looking simple, these questions are not answered by the established economic theory, which usually views firms as given, and treats them as black boxes without any internal structure.

The First World War period saw a change of emphasis in economic theory away from industry-level analysis which mainly included analysing markets to analysis at the level of the firm, as it became increasingly clear that perfect competition was no longer an adequate model of how firms behaved. Economic theory till then had focussed on trying to understand markets alone and there had been little study on understanding why firms or organisations exist.

a. Khazzoom-Brookes postulate
b. Policy Ineffectiveness Proposition
c. Technology gap
d. Theory of the firm

Chapter 13. Money, Banking, and the Federal Reserve

21. The _____, a United States federal financial statute law passed in 1980, gave the Federal Reserve greater control over non-member banks.

- It forced all banks to abide by the Fed's rules.
- It allowed banks to merge.
- It removed the power of the Federal Reserve Board of Governors under the Glass-Steagall Act and Regulation Q to set the interest rates of savings accounts.
- It raised the deposit insurance of US banks and credit unions from $40,000 to $100,000.
- It allowed credit unions and savings and loans to offer checkable deposits.
- Allowed institutions to charge any interest rates they chose.

a. Cash flow loan
b. Capital guarantee
c. Market-based instruments
d. Depository Institutions Deregulation and Monetary Control Act

22. _____ is the removal or simplification of government rules and regulations that constrain the operation of market forces. _____ does not mean elimination of laws against fraud, but eliminating or reducing government control of how business is done, thereby moving toward a more free market.

The stated rationale for '_____' is often that fewer and simpler regulations will lead to a raised level of competitiveness, therefore higher productivity, more efficiency and lower prices overall.

a. Secular basis
b. Macroeconomic policy instruments
c. Deregulation
d. Fundamental psychological law

23. In banking, _____ are bank reserves in excess of the reserve requirement set by a central bank (in the United States, the Federal Reserve System, called the Fed; in Canada, the Bank of Canada.) They are reserves of cash more than the required amounts. Holding _____ is generally considered costly and uneconomical as no interest is earned on the excess amount.

a. Universal bank
b. Origination fee
c. Excess reserves
d. Annual percentage rate

24. The _____ is a United States government corporation created by the Glass-Steagall Act of 1933. It provides deposit insurance, which guarantees the safety of deposits in member banks, currently up to $250,000 per depositor per bank. Funds in non-interest bearing transaction accounts are fully insured, with no limit, under the temporary Transaction Account Guarantee Program.

a. Great Leap Forward
b. Foreign direct investment
c. Luxembourg Income Study
d. Federal Deposit Insurance Corporation

25. In the United States, _____ are overnight borrowings by banks to maintain their bank reserves at the Federal Reserve. Banks keep reserves at Federal Reserve Banks to meet their reserve requirements and to clear financial transactions. Transactions in the _____ market enable depository institutions with reserve balances in excess of reserve requirements to lend reserves to institutions with reserve deficiencies.

a. Federal Reserve Transparency Act
b. Federal funds
c. Term auction facility
d. Federal funds rate

26. In the United States, the _____ is the interest rate at which private depository institutions (mostly banks) lend balances (federal funds) at the Federal Reserve to other depository institutions, usually overnight. It is the interest rate banks charge each other for loans. Changing the target rate is one way the Chairman of the Federal Reserve can influence the supply of money in the U.S. economy..
   a. Federal banking
   b. Term auction facility
   c. Monetary Policy Report to the Congress
   d. Federal funds rate

27. _____, in law and economics, is a form of risk management primarily used to hedge against the risk of a contingent loss. _____ is defined as the equitable transfer of the risk of a loss, from one entity to another, in exchange for a premium, and can be thought of as a guaranteed small loss to prevent a large, possibly devastating loss. An insurer is a company selling the _____; an insured or policyholder is the person or entity buying the _____.
   a. ACCRA Cost of Living Index
   b. Insurance
   c. AD-IA Model
   d. ACEA agreement

28. The _____ is a bank regulation that sets the minimum reserves each bank must hold to customer deposits and notes. It would normally be in the form of fiat currency stored in a bank vault (vault cash), or with a central bank.

The reserve ratio is sometimes used as a tool in the monetary policy, influencing the country's economy, borrowing, and interest rates.

   a. Fractional-reserve banking
   b. Private money
   c. Probability of default
   d. Reserve requirement

29. A security is a fungible, negotiable instrument representing financial value. _____ are broadly categorized into debt _____; equity _____, e.g., common stocks; and derivative (finance) contracts such as forwards, futures, options and swaps. The company or other entity issuing the security is called the issuer.
   a. Pass-Through Certificates
   b. Red herring prospectus
   c. Settlement risk
   d. Securities

30. A United States Treasury security is a government debt issued by the United States Department of the Treasury through the Bureau of the Public Debt. Treasury securities are the debt financing instruments of the United States Federal government, and they are often referred to simply as Treasuries. There are four types of marketable treasury securities: _____, Treasury notes, Treasury bonds, and Treasury Inflation Protected Securities (TIPS.)
   a. Lawcards
   b. Treasury bills
   c. Labour battalions
   d. Debt to Assets

31. _____ is a term applied in many countries to a reference interest rate used by banks. The term originally indicated the rate of interest at which banks lent to favored customers, i.e., those with high credibility, though this is no longer always the case. Some variable interest rates may be expressed as a percentage above or below _____.
   a. Repo Rate
   b. Transactional account
   c. Capital requirement
   d. Prime rate

Chapter 13. Money, Banking, and the Federal Reserve

32. Discounting is a financial mechanism in which a debtor obtains the right to delay payments to a creditor, for a defined period of time, in exchange for a charge or fee. Essentially, the party that owes money in the present purchases the right to delay the payment until some future date. The _____, or charge, is simply the difference between the original amount owed in the present and the amount that has to be paid in the future to settle the debt.

a. Discount
b. Reliability theory
c. Certified Risk Manager
d. Reinsurance

33. The _____ is an interest rate a central bank charges depository institutions that borrow reserves from it.

The term _____ has two meanings:

- the same as interest rate; the term 'discount' does not refer to the meaning of the word, but to the purpose of using the quantity, such as computations of present value, e.g. net present value or discounted cash flow

- the annual effective _____, which is the annual interest divided by the capital including that interest; this rate is lower than the interest rate; it corresponds to using the value after a year as the nominal value, and seeing the initial value as the nominal value minus a discount; it is used for Treasury Bills and similar financial instruments

The annual effective _____ is the annual interest divided by the capital including that interest, which is the interest rate divided by 100% plus the interest rate. It is the annual discount factor to be applied to the future cash flow, to find the discount, subtracted from a future value to find the value one year earlier.

For example, suppose there is a government bond that sells for $95 and pays $100 in a year's time.

a. Stochastic volatility
b. Discount rate
c. Perpetuity
d. Johansen test

34. The cost advantages of using _____ include:

- Reconciling conflicting preferences of lenders and borrowers

- Risk aversion- intermediaries help spread out and decrease the risks

- Economies of scale- using _____ reduces the costs of lending and borrowing

- Economies of scope- intermediaries concentrate on the demands of the lenders and borrowers and are able to enhance their products and services (use same inputs to produce different outputs)

_____ include:

- Banks
- Building societies
- Credit unions
- Financial advisers or brokers
- Insurance companies
- Collective investment schemes
- Pension funds

Financial institutions (intermediaries) perform the vital role of bringing together those economic agents with surplus funds who want to lend, with those with a shortage of funds who want to borrow.

In doing this they offer the major benefits of maturity and risk transformation. It is possible for this to be done by direct contact between the ultimate borrowers, but there are major cost disadvantages of direct finance.

Indeed, one explanation of the existence of specialist _____ is that they have a related (cost) advantage in offering financial services, which not only enables them to make profit, but also raises the overall efficiency of the economy.

a. Financial intermediaries
c. SICAV
b. Collective investment scheme
d. Broker-dealer

35. In business, _____ is the total liabilitiess minus total outside assets of an individual or a company. For a company, this is called shareholders' prefernce and may be referred to as book value. _____ is stated as at a particular year in time.
    a. Post earnings announcement drift
    c. Bond credit rating
    b. Sinking fund
    d. Net worth

36. _____ is a fee paid on borrowed assets. It is the price paid for the use of borrowed money , or, money earned by deposited funds . Assets that are sometimes lent with _____ include money, shares, consumer goods through hire purchase, major assets such as aircraft, and even entire factories in finance lease arrangements.
    a. Internal debt
    c. Insolvency
    b. Asset protection
    d. Interest

37. An _____ is the price a borrower pays for the use of money they do not own, for instance a small company might borrow from a bank to kick start their business, and the return a lender receives for deferring the use of funds, by lending it to the borrower. _____s are normally expressed as a percentage rate over the period of one year.

_____s targets are also a vital tool of monetary policy and are used to control variables like investment, inflation, and unemployment.

Chapter 13. Money, Banking, and the Federal Reserve

a. Enterprise value
b. Arrow-Debreu model
c. ACCRA Cost of Living Index
d. Interest rate

38. The _____ or gross domestic income (GDI), a basic measure of an economy's economic performance, is the market value of all final goods and services produced within the borders of a nation in a year. _____ can be defined in three ways, all of which are conceptually identical. First, it is equal to the total expenditures for all final goods and services produced within the country in a stipulated period of time (usually a 365-day year.)
   a. Market structure
   b. Monopolistic competition
   c. Countercyclical
   d. Gross domestic product

39. The _____ , a component of the Federal Reserve System, is charged under United States law with overseeing the nation's open market operations. It is the Federal Reserve Committee that makes key decisions about interest rates and the growth jam of the United States money supply. It is the principal organ of United States national monetary policy.
   a. Primary Dealer Credit Facility
   b. Federal Reserve Transparency Act
   c. Fed Funds Probability
   d. Federal Open Market Committee

40. The Federal Reserve System (also the Federal Reserve; informally The Fed) is the central banking system of the United States. Created in 1913 by the enactment of the Federal Reserve Act (signed by Woodrow Wilson), it is a quasi-public and quasi-private (government entity with private components) banking system that comprises (1) the presidentially appointed Board of Governors of the Federal Reserve System in Washington, D.C.; (2) the Federal Open Market Committee; (3) twelve regional _____ located in major cities throughout the nation acting as fiscal agents for the U.S. Treasury, each with its own nine-member board of directors; (4) numerous other private U.S. member banks, which subscribe to required amounts of non-transferable stock in their regional _____; and (5) various advisory councils. Since February 2006, Ben Bernanke has served as the Chairman of the Board of Governors of the Federal Reserve System.
   a. Federal Reserve Banks
   b. Federal Open Market Committee
   c. Federal funds
   d. Fed Funds Probability

41. In economics, the _____ is the term used to refer to the environment in which bonds are bought and sold between a central bank ' its regulated banks. It is not a free market process.

- To intervene in the 'business cycle', a central bank may choose to go into the _____ and buy or sell government bonds, which is known as _____ operations to increase reserves.

   a. Open Market
   b. Outside money
   c. ACCRA Cost of Living Index
   d. Inside money

42. In economics, the _____ is a term relating to the money supply, the amount of money in the economy. The _____ comprises only coins, paper money, and commercial banks' reserves with the central bank. Broader measures of the money supply include the public's bank deposits .
   a. Monetary base
   b. Chartalism
   c. Monetary economy
   d. Quantum economics

43. In economics, _____ is the total amount of money available in an economy at a particular point in time. There are several ways to define 'money', but standard measures usually include currency in circulation and demand deposits.

_____ data are recorded and published, usually by the government or the central bank of the country.

a. Veil of money
c. Neutrality of money
b. Velocity of money
d. Money supply

44. _____ are the means of implementing monetary policy by which a central bank controls its national money supply by buying and selling government securities, or other financial instruments. Monetary targets, such as interest rates or exchange rates, are used to guide this implementation.

Since most money is now in the form of electronic records, rather than paper records such as banknotes, _____ are conducted simply by electronically increasing or decreasing ('crediting' or 'debiting') the amount of money that a bank has, e.g., in its reserve account at the central bank, in exchange for a bank selling or buying a financial instrument.

a. ACEA agreement
c. AD-IA Model
b. ACCRA Cost of Living Index
d. Open market operations

45. _____ is the process by which the government, central bank (ii) availability of money, and (iii) cost of money or rate of interest, in order to attain a set of objectives oriented towards the growth and stability of the economy. Monetary theory provides insight into how to craft optimal _____.

_____ is referred to as either being an expansionary policy where an expansionary policy increases the total supply of money in the economy, and a contractionary policy decreases the total money supply.

a. 1921 recession
c. 130-30 fund
b. 100-year flood
d. Monetary policy

46. A _____ occurs when a bank is unable to meet its obligations to its depositors or other creditors. More specifically, a bank fails economically when the market value of its assets declines to a value that is less than the market value of its liabilities. As such, the bank is unable to fulfill the demands of all of its depositors on time.

a. Bank failure
c. Lombard Club
b. Concentration account
d. Transactional account

47. The most common mechanism used to measure this increase in the money supply is typically called the _____. It calculates the maximum amount of money that an initial deposit can be expanded to with a given reserve ratio - such a factor is called a multiplier.

The _____, m, is the inverse of the reserve requirement, R:

$$m = \frac{1}{R}$$

This formula stems from the fact that the sum of the 'amount loaned out' column above can be expressed mathematically as a geometric series with a common ratio of 1 − R.

a. Flow to Equity-Approach
c. Fixed-income arbitrage
b. Money multiplier
d. Kibbutz volunteers

48. _____ is the prospect that a party insulated from risk may behave differently from the way it would behave if it were fully exposed to the risk. In insurance, _____ that occurs without conscious or malicious action is called morale hazard.

_____ is related to information asymmetry, a situation in which one party in a transaction has more information than another.

a. 130-30 fund
c. 100-year flood
b. 1921 recession
d. Moral hazard

Chapter 14. Monetary Policy and Price Stability

1. _____ is monetary policy that seeks to increase the size of the money supply. In most nations, monetary policy is controlled by either a central bank or a finance ministry

Neoclassical and Keynesian economics significantly differ on the effects and effectiveness of monetary policy on influencing the real economy; there is no clear consensus on how monetary policy affects real economic variables (aggregate output or income, employment.) Both economic schools accept that monetary policy affects monetary variables (price levels, interest rates.)

a. AD-IA Model
b. ACEA agreement
c. Expansionary monetary policy
d. ACCRA Cost of Living Index

2. _____ in economics and business is the result of an exchange and from that trade we assign a numerical monetary value to a good, service or asset. If Alice trades Bob 4 apples for an orange, the _____ of an orange is 4 apples. Inversely, the _____ of an apple is 1/4 oranges.

a. Price
b. Premium pricing
c. Price war
d. Price book

3. In economics, _____ is a rise in the general level of prices of goods and services in an economy over a period of time. When the general price level rises, each unit of currency buys fewer goods and services; consequently, _____ is also a decline in the real value of money--a loss of purchasing power in the medium of exchange which is also the monetary unit of account in the economy. A chief measure of general price-level _____ is the general _____ rate, which is the percentage change in a general price index (normally the Consumer Price Index) over time.

a. Opportunity cost
b. Energy economics
c. Inflation
d. Economic

4. _____ is the process by which the government, central bank (ii) availability of money, and (iii) cost of money or rate of interest, in order to attain a set of objectives oriented towards the growth and stability of the economy. Monetary theory provides insight into how to craft optimal _____.

_____ is referred to as either being an expansionary policy where an expansionary policy increases the total supply of money in the economy, and a contractionary policy decreases the total money supply.

a. 100-year flood
b. 130-30 fund
c. 1921 recession
d. Monetary policy

5. _____ is monetary policy that seeks to reduce the size of the money supply. They are fiscal policies, like lower spending and higher taxes, that reduce economic growth. In most nations, monetary policy is controlled by either a central bank or a finance ministry.

a. Monetary policy of Sweden
b. Shadow Open Market Committee
c. Contractionary monetary policy
d. Money creation

6. In economics, _____ is the total amount of money available in an economy at a particular point in time. There are several ways to define 'money', but standard measures usually include currency in circulation and demand deposits.

_____ data are recorded and published, usually by the government or the central bank of the country.

Chapter 14. Monetary Policy and Price Stability

a. Neutrality of money
b. Velocity of money
c. Veil of money
d. Money supply

7. In economics, the _____ is the term used to refer to the environment in which bonds are bought and sold between a central bank ' its regulated banks. It is not a free market process.

- To intervene in the 'business cycle', a central bank may choose to go into the _____ and buy or sell government bonds, which is known as _____ operations to increase reserves.

a. ACCRA Cost of Living Index
b. Outside money
c. Inside money
d. Open Market

8. The _____ is an independent, monetarist economic analysis committee founded in 1973 by Profs. Karl Brunner, from the University of Rochester, and Allan Meltzer, from Carnegie Mellon University of which it is often critical. Its members are drawn both from academia and the private sector.

a. Second-round effect
b. Shadow Open Market Committee
c. Lombard credit
d. Monetary policy of Sweden

9. _____ is a fee paid on borrowed assets. It is the price paid for the use of borrowed money , or, money earned by deposited funds . Assets that are sometimes lent with _____ include money, shares, consumer goods through hire purchase, major assets such as aircraft, and even entire factories in finance lease arrangements.

a. Insolvency
b. Internal debt
c. Asset protection
d. Interest

10. An _____ is the price a borrower pays for the use of money they do not own, for instance a small company might borrow from a bank to kick start their business, and the return a lender receives for deferring the use of funds, by lending it to the borrower. _____s are normally expressed as a percentage rate over the period of one year.

_____s targets are also a vital tool of monetary policy and are used to control variables like investment, inflation, and unemployment.

a. ACCRA Cost of Living Index
b. Arrow-Debreu model
c. Enterprise value
d. Interest rate

11. Economics:

- _____,the desire to own something and the ability to pay for it
- _____ curve,a graphic representation of a _____ schedule
- _____ deposit, the money in checking accounts
- _____ pull theory,the theory that inflation occurs when _____ for goods and services exceeds existing supplies
- _____ schedule,a table that lists the quantity of a good a person will buy it each different price
- _____ side economics,the school of economics at believes government spending and tax cuts open economy by raising _____

a. Variability
b. McKesson ' Robbins scandal
c. Production
d. Demand

12. The _____ is the desired holding of money balances in the form of cash or bank deposits.

Money is dominated as store of value by interest bearing assets. However, money is necessary to carry out transactions, or in other words, it provides liquidity.

a. Borrowing base
b. Conglomerate merger
c. Market neutral
d. Demand for money

13. In finance, the _____ is the global financial market for short-term borrowing and lending. It provides short-term liquidity funding for the global financial system. The _____ is where short-term obligations such as Treasury bills, commercial paper and bankers' acceptances are bought and sold.

a. Deferred compensation
b. T-Model
c. Consignment stock
d. Money market

14. In economics, economic equilibrium is simply a state of the world where economic forces are balanced and in the absence of external influences the (equilibrium) values of economic variables will not change. It is the point at which quantity demanded and quantity supplied are equal. _____, for example, refers to a condition where a market price is established through competition such that the amount of goods or services sought by buyers is equal to the amount of goods or services produced by sellers.

a. Regulated market
b. Marketization
c. Product-Market Growth Matrix
d. Market equilibrium

15. In economics, _____ is when quantity demanded is more than quantity supplied. See Economic shortage.

a. Excess demand
b. ACCRA Cost of Living Index
c. AD-IA Model
d. ACEA agreement

16. In economics, _____ is when quantity supplied is more than quantity demanded. .

a. Illicit financial flows
b. Effective unemployment rate
c. Economic Value Creation
d. Excess supply

17. In economics, the _____ is the relation:

$$M \cdot V = P \cdot Q$$

where, for a given period,

M is the total amount of money in circulation on average in an economy.
V is the velocity of money, that is the average frequency with which a unit of money is spent.
P is the price level.

a. ACCRA Cost of Living Index
b. Equation of exchange
c. Open market
d. Outside money

18. The _____ is the average frequency with which a unit of money is spent in a specific period of time. Velocity associates the amount of economic activity associated with a given money supply. When the period is understood, the velocity may be present as a pure number; otherwise it should be given as a pure number over time.

a. Money supply
b. Neutrality of money
c. Velocity of money
d. Chartalism

94 Chapter 14. Monetary Policy and Price Stability

19. A _____ is:

- Rewrite _____, in generative grammar and computer science
- Standardization, a formal and widely-accepted statement, fact, definition, or qualification
- Operation, a determinate _____ for performing a mathematical operation and obtaining a certain result (Mathematics, Logic)
    - Unary operation
    - Binary operation
- _____ of inference, a function from sets of formulae to formulae (Mathematics, Logic)
- _____ of thumb, principle with broad application that is not intended to be strictly accurate or reliable for every situation. Also often simply referred to as a _____
- Moral, an atomic element of a moral code for guiding choices in human behavior
- Heuristic, a quantized '_____' which shows a tendency or probability for successful function
- A regulation, as in sports
- A Production _____, as in computer science
- Procedural law, a _____ set governing the application of laws to cases
    - A law, which may informally be called a '_____'
    - A court ruling, a decision by a court
- In the U.S. Government, a regulation mandated by Congress, but written or expanded upon by the Executive Branch.
- Norm (sociology), an informal but widely accepted _____, concept, truth, definition, or qualification (social norms, legal norms, coding norms)
- Norm (philosophy), a kind of sentence or a reason to act, feel or believe
- 'Rulership' is the concept of governance by a government:
    - Military _____, governance by a military body
    - Monastic _____, a collection of precepts that guides the life of monks or nuns in a religious order where the superior holds the place of Christ
- Slide _____

- '_____,' a song by Ayumi Hamasaki
- '_____,' a song by rapper Nas
- '_____s,' an album by the band The Whitest Boy Alive
- _____s: Pyaar Ka Superhit Formula, a 2003 Bollywood film
- ruler, an instrument for measuring lengths
- _____, a component of an astrolabe, circumferator or similar instrument
- The _____s, a bestselling self-help book
- _____ Project (Run Up-to-date Linux Everywhere), a project that aims to use up-to-date Linux software on old PCs
- _____ engine, a software system that helps managing business _____s
- Ja _____, a hip hop artist
    - R.U.L.E., a 2005 greatest hits album by rapper Ja _____
- '_____s,' a KMFDM song

a. Technocracy
b. Demand
c. Procter ' Gamble
d. Rule

Chapter 14. Monetary Policy and Price Stability

20. In economics, the _____ of money is a theory emphasizing the positive relationship of overall prices or the nominal value of expenditures to the quantity of money.

It is the mainstream economic theory of the price level. Alternative theories include the real bills doctrine and the more recent fiscal theory of the price level.

a. Quantity theory
b. Romer Model
c. Real business cycle
d. Dishoarding

21. In economics, the _____ is a theory emphasizing the positive relationship of overall prices or the nominal value of expenditures to the quantity of money.

It is the mainstream economic theory of the price level. Alternative theories include the real bills doctrine and the more recent fiscal theory of the price level.

a. Fundamental psychological law
b. Consumer spending
c. Quantity theory of money
d. Microsimulation

22. _____ was an American economist, statistician and public intellectual, and a recipient of the Nobel Memorial Prize in Economic Sciences. He is best known among scholars for his theoretical and empirical research, especially consumption analysis, monetary history and theory, and for his demonstration of the complexity of stabilization policy. A global public followed his restatement of a political philosophy that insisted on minimizing the role of government in favor of the private sector.

a. Adam Smith
b. Adolf Hitler
c. Adolph Fischer
d. Milton Friedman

23. _____ is the view within monetary economics that variation in the money supply has major influences on national output in the short run and the price level over longer periods and that objectives of monetary policy are best met by targeting the growth rate of the money supply.

_____ today is mainly associated with the work of Milton Friedman, who was among the generation of economists to accept Keynesian economics and then criticize it on his own terms. Friedman and Anna Schwartz wrote an influential book, Monetary History of the United States 1867-1960, and argued that 'inflation is always and everywhere a monetary phenomenon.' Friedman advocated a central bank policy aimed at keeping the supply and demand for money at equilibrium, as measured by growth in productivity and demand.

a. Complexity economics
b. Marginal revenue productivity theory of wages
c. Historical school of economics
d. Monetarism

24. Market _____ is a business, economics or investment term that refers to an asset's ability to be easily converted through an act of buying or selling without causing a significant movement in the price and with minimum loss of value. Money, or cash on hand, is the most liquid asset. An act of exchange of a less liquid asset with a more liquid asset is called liquidation.

a. 130-30 fund
b. 100-year flood
c. 1921 recession
d. Liquidity

Chapter 14. Monetary Policy and Price Stability

25. The term _____ is used in macroeconomics to refer to a situation where a country's nominal interest rate has been lowered nearly to or equal to zero to avoid a recession, but the liquidity in the market created by these low interest rates does not stimulate the economy to full employment. In this situation, any further increase in the money supply will not stimulate the economy any further. This is because any further injection of liquidity will no longer lower the nominal interest rate, as the nominal interest rate cannot drop below zero.
    a. Macroeconomic models
    b. Robertson lag
    c. Minimum wage
    d. Liquidity trap

26. The Federal Reserve System (also the Federal Reserve; informally The Fed) is the central banking system of the United States. Created in 1913 by the enactment of the Federal Reserve Act (signed by Woodrow Wilson), it is a quasi-public and quasi-private (government entity with private components) banking system that comprises (1) the presidentially appointed Board of Governors of the Federal Reserve System in Washington, D.C.; (2) the Federal Open Market Committee; (3) twelve regional _____ located in major cities throughout the nation acting as fiscal agents for the U.S. Treasury, each with its own nine-member board of directors; (4) numerous other private U.S. member banks, which subscribe to required amounts of non-transferable stock in their regional _____; and (5) various advisory councils. Since February 2006, Ben Bernanke has served as the Chairman of the Board of Governors of the Federal Reserve System.
    a. Federal funds
    b. Federal Open Market Committee
    c. Fed Funds Probability
    d. Federal Reserve Banks

27. In the United States, _____ are overnight borrowings by banks to maintain their bank reserves at the Federal Reserve. Banks keep reserves at Federal Reserve Banks to meet their reserve requirements and to clear financial transactions. Transactions in the _____ market enable depository institutions with reserve balances in excess of reserve requirements to lend reserves to institutions with reserve deficiencies.
    a. Federal funds
    b. Federal Reserve Transparency Act
    c. Federal funds rate
    d. Term auction facility

28. In the United States, the _____ is the interest rate at which private depository institutions (mostly banks) lend balances (federal funds) at the Federal Reserve to other depository institutions, usually overnight. It is the interest rate banks charge each other for loans. Changing the target rate is one way the Chairman of the Federal Reserve can influence the supply of money in the U.S. economy..
    a. Monetary Policy Report to the Congress
    b. Term auction facility
    c. Federal banking
    d. Federal funds rate

29. _____ are the means of implementing monetary policy by which a central bank controls its national money supply by buying and selling government securities, or other financial instruments. Monetary targets, such as interest rates or exchange rates, are used to guide this implementation.

Since most money is now in the form of electronic records, rather than paper records such as banknotes, _____ are conducted simply by electronically increasing or decreasing ('crediting' or 'debiting') the amount of money that a bank has, e.g., in its reserve account at the central bank, in exchange for a bank selling or buying a financial instrument.

    a. ACEA agreement
    b. Open market operations
    c. ACCRA Cost of Living Index
    d. AD-IA Model

Chapter 14. Monetary Policy and Price Stability

30. In finance and economics _____ or nominal rate of interest refers to the rate of interest before adjustment for inflation (in contrast with the real interest rate); or, for interest rates 'as stated' without adjustment for the full effect of compounding (also referred to as the nominal annual rate.) An interest rate is called nominal if the frequency of compounding (e.g. a month) is not identical to the basic time unit (normally a year.)

The real interest rate includes compensation for the lender's lost value due to inflation, whereas the _____ excludes inflation.

a. Risk-free interest rate
c. Nominal interest rate
b. Fixed interest
d. London Interbank Offered Rate

31. The '_____' is approximately the nominal interest rate minus the inflation rate Since the inflation rate over the course of a loan is not known initially, volatility in inflation represents a risk to both the lender and the borrower.

In economics and finance, an individual who lends money for repayment at a later point in time expects to be compensated for the time value of money, or not having the use of that money while it is lent.

a. Core inflation
c. Reflation
b. Real interest rate
d. Cost-push inflation

32. A _____, reserve bank, or monetary authority is the entity responsible for the monetary policy of a country or of a group of member states. It is a bank that can lend money to other banks in times of need. Its primary responsibility is to maintain the stability of the national currency and money supply, but more active duties include controlling subsidized-loan interest rates, and acting as a lender of last resort to the banking sector during times of financial crisis (private banks often being integral to the national financial system.)

a. 100-year flood
c. Central Bank
b. 130-30 fund
d. 1921 recession

33. The _____ is one of the world's most important central banks, responsible for monetary policy covering the 16 member States of the Eurozone. It was established by the European Union (EU) in 1998 with its headquarters in Frankfurt, Germany.

The predecessor to the _____ was the European Monetary Institute .

a. ACCRA Cost of Living Index
c. AD-IA Model
b. European Central Bank
d. ACEA agreement

Chapter 15. Into the International Marketplace

1. In economics, the _____ measures the payments that flow between any individual country and all other countries. It is used to summarize all international economic transactions for that country during a specific time period, usually a year. The _____ is determined by the country's exports and imports of goods, services, and financial capital, as well as financial transfers.
   a. Gross domestic product per barrel
   b. Skyscraper Index
   c. Gross world product
   d. Balance of payments

2. The _____ is the difference between the monetary value of exports and imports in an economy over a certain period of time. It is the relationship between a nation's imports and exports. A positive _____ is known as a trade surplus and consists of exporting more than is imported; a negative _____ is known as a trade deficit or, informally, a trade gap.
   a. Marginal propensity to import
   b. Rational expectations
   c. SIMIC
   d. Balance of trade

3. In economics, the _____ is one of the two primary components of the balance of payments, the other being the capital account. It is the sum of the balance of trade (exports minus imports of goods and services), net factor income (such as interest and dividends) and net transfer payments (such as foreign aid.)

$$\text{Current account} = \text{Balance of trade}$$
$$+ \text{Net factor income from abroad}$$
$$+ \text{Net unilateral transfers from abroad}$$

   The _____ balance is one of two major metrics of the nature of a country's foreign trade (the other being the net capital outflow.)

   a. Compensation of employees
   b. Gross private domestic investment
   c. National Income and Product Accounts
   d. Current account

4. In economics, an _____ is any good or commodity, transported from one country to another country in a legitimate fashion, typically for use in trade. _____ goods or services are provided to foreign consumers by domestic producers. _____ is an important part of international trade.
   a. AD-IA Model
   b. ACEA agreement
   c. ACCRA Cost of Living Index
   d. Export

5. In economics, an _____ is any good (e.g. a commodity) or service brought into one country from another country in a legitimate fashion, typically for use in trade. It is a good that is brought in from another country for sale. _____ goods or services are provided to domestic consumers by foreign producers. An _____ in the receiving country is an export to the sending country.
   a. Incoterms
   b. Economic integration
   c. Import quota
   d. Import

6. _____ is exchange of capital, goods, and services across international borders or territories. In most countries, it represents a significant share of gross domestic product (GDP.) While _____ has been present throughout much of history, its economic, social, and political importance has been on the rise in recent centuries.

Chapter 15. Into the International Marketplace

a. Incoterms
b. Intra-industry trade
c. Import license
d. International trade

7. The balance of trade (or net exports, sometimes symbolized as NX) is the difference between the monetary value of exports and imports in an economy over a certain period of time. It is the relationship between a nation's imports and exports. A favorable balance of trade is known as a trade surplus and consists of exporting more than is imported; an unfavorable balance of trade is known as a _____ or, informally, a trade gap.
a. Computational economic
b. Demographics of India
c. Complementary asset
d. Trade deficit

8. _____ is a term used in accounting relating to the increase in value of an asset. In this sense it is the reverse of depreciation, which measures the fall in value of assets over their normal life-time.

_____ is a rise of a currency in a floating exchange rate.

a. Appreciation
b. AD-IA Model
c. ACCRA Cost of Living Index
d. ACEA agreement

9. _____ is money accepted for exchange of goods in an economy. The prevalence of one money over another arises, usually, when a government designates through decrees that the government shall accept only particular notes and coins in payment for taxes. Typically, money of _____ consists of stamped coins and minted paper bills.
a. Currency
b. Local currency
c. Security thread
d. Totnes pound

10. A _____ is the transfer of wealth from one party (such as a person or company) to another. A _____ is usually made in exchange for the provision of goods, services or both, or to fulfill a legal obligation.

The simplest and oldest form of _____ is barter, the exchange of one good or service for another.

a. Social gravity
b. Going concern
c. Soft count
d. Payment

11. The _____ or gross domestic income (GDI), a basic measure of an economy's economic performance, is the market value of all final goods and services produced within the borders of a nation in a year. _____ can be defined in three ways, all of which are conceptually identical. First, it is equal to the total expenditures for all final goods and services produced within the country in a stipulated period of time (usually a 365-day year.)
a. Monopolistic competition
b. Countercyclical
c. Market structure
d. Gross domestic product

12. Capital intensity is the term in economics for the amount of fixed or real capital present in relation to other factors of production, especially labor. At the level of either a production process or the aggregate economy, it may be estimated by the capital/labor ratio, such as from the points along a capital/labor isoquant.

Since the use of tools and machinery makes labor more effective, rising capital intensity (or 'capital deepening') pushes up the productivity of labor, so a society that is more _____ tends to have a higher standard of living over the long run than one with low capital intensity.

Chapter 15. Into the International Marketplace

a. Wealth inequality in the United States
b. Capital flight
c. Capital intensive
d. Modigliani-Miller theorem

13. _____ to the arrival of new individuals into a habitat or population. It is a biological concept and is important in population ecology, differentiated from emigration and migration.

_____ is a modern phenomenon.

a. Immigration
b. AD-IA Model
c. ACCRA Cost of Living Index
d. ACEA agreement

14. In finance, the _____s between two currencies specifies how much one currency is worth in terms of the other. It is the value of a foreign natione;s currency in terms of the home natione;s currency. For example an _____ of 102 Japanese yen to the United States dollar means that JPY 102 is worth the same as USD 1.

a. Exchange rate
b. Interbank market
c. ACEA agreement
d. ACCRA Cost of Living Index

15. The _____ is where currency trading takes place. It is where banks and other official institutions facilitate the buying and selling of foreign currencies. FX transactions typically involve one party purchasing a quantity of one currency in exchange for paying a quantity of another.

a. Floating currency
b. Currency swap
c. Covered interest arbitrage
d. Foreign exchange market

16. _____ is a type of risk faced by investors, corporations, and governments. It is a risk that can be understood and managed with proper aforethought and investment.

Broadly, _____ refers to the complications businesses and governments may face as a result of what are commonly referred to as political decisions--or e;any political change that alters the expected outcome and value of a given economic action by changing the probability of achieving business objectives.e; .

a. Pull to par
b. Capital adequacy ratio
c. Black-Derman-Toy model
d. Political risk

17. In economics, economic equilibrium is simply a state of the world where economic forces are balanced and in the absence of external influences the (equilibrium) values of economic variables will not change. It is the point at which quantity demanded and quantity supplied are equal. _____, for example, refers to a condition where a market price is established through competition such that the amount of goods or services sought by buyers is equal to the amount of goods or services produced by sellers.

a. Marketization
b. Product-Market Growth Matrix
c. Market equilibrium
d. Regulated market

18. _____ is a term used in accounting, economics and finance to spread the cost of an asset over the span of several years.

In simple words we can say that _____ is the reduction in the value of an asset due to usage, passage of time, wear and tear, technological outdating or obsolescence, depletion, inadequacy, rot, rust, decay or other such factors.

In accounting, _____ is a term used to describe any method of attributing the historical or purchase cost of an asset across its useful life, roughly corresponding to normal wear and tear.

a. Salvage value
b. Historical cost
c. Net income per employee
d. Depreciation

19. _____ is the loss of value of a country's currency with respect to one or more foreign reference currencies, typically in a floating exchange rate system. It is most often used for the unofficial increase of the exchange rate due to market forces, though sometimes it appears interchangeably with devaluation. Its opposite is called appreciation.

a. Quote currency
b. Fed Shreds
c. Currency depreciation
d. Hero Card

20. _____ refers to a business or organization attempting to acquire goods or services to accomplish the goals of the enterprise. Though there are several organizations that attempt to set standards in the _____ process, processes can vary greatly between organizations. Typically the word '_____' is not used interchangeably with the word 'procurement', since procurement typically includes Expediting, Supplier Quality, and Traffic and Logistics (T'L) in addition to _____.

a. Free port
b. 100-year flood
c. 130-30 fund
d. Purchasing

21. A _____, sometimes called a pegged exchange rate, is a type of exchange rate regime wherein a currency's value is matched to the value of another single currency or to a basket of other currencies such as gold.

A _____ is usually used to stabilize the value of a currency, vis-a-vis the currency it is pegged to. This facilitates trade and investments between the two countries, and is especially useful for small economies where external trade forms a large part of their GDP.

a. Fixed exchange rate
b. Leading indicators
c. Monetary economics
d. Law of supply

22. A _____ or a flexible exchange rate is a type of exchange rate regime wherein a currency's value is allowed to fluctuate according to the foreign exchange market. A currency that uses a _____ is known as a floating currency. The opposite of a _____ is a fixed exchange rate.

a. Floating currency
b. Foreign exchange market
c. Trade Weighted US dollar Index
d. Floating exchange rate

23. In cases of extreme appreciation or depreciation, a central bank will normally intervene to stabilize the currency. Thus, the exchange rate regimes of floating currencies may more technically be known as a _____. A central bank might, for instance, allow a currency price to float freely between an upper and lower bound, a price 'ceiling' and 'floor'.

a. Triangular arbitrage
b. Foreign exchange reserves
c. Continuous linked settlement
d. Managed float

Chapter 15. Into the International Marketplace

24. A fixed exchange rate, sometimes called a _____, is a type of exchange rate regime wherein a currency's value is matched to the value of another single currency or to a basket of other currencies such as gold.

A fixed exchange rate is usually used to stabilize the value of a currency, vis-a-vis the currency it is pegged to. This facilitates trade and investments between the two countries, and is especially useful for small economies where external trade forms a large part of their GDP.

a. Leading indicators
b. Recession
c. Mainstream economics
d. Pegged exchange rate

25. A _____ is a monetary authority which is required to maintain a fixed exchange rate with a foreign currency. This policy objective requires the conventional objectives of a central bank to be subordinated to the exchange rate target.

The main qualities of an orthodox _____ are:

- A _____'s foreign currency reserves must be sufficient to ensure that all holders of its notes and coins (and all banks creditor of a Reserve Account at the _____) can convert them into the reserve currency (usually 110-115% of the monetary base M0.)
- A _____ maintains absolute, unlimited convertibility between its notes and coins and the currency against which they are pegged (the anchor currency), at a fixed rate of exchange, with no restrictions on current-account or capital-account transactions.
- A _____ only earns profit from interests on foreign reserves (less the expense of note-issuing), and does not engage in forward-exchange transactions. These foreign reserves exist (1) because local notes have been issued in exchange, or (2) because commercial banks must by regulation deposit a minimum reserve at the _____. (1) generates a seignorage revenue. (2) is the revenue on minimum reserves (revenue of investment activities less cost of minimum reserves remuneration)
- A _____ has no discretionary powers to effect monetary policy and does not lend to the government. Governments cannot print money, and can only tax or borrow to meet their spending commitments.
- A _____ does not act as a lender of last resort to commercial banks, and does not regulate reserve requirements.
- A _____ does not attempt to manipulate interest rates by establishing a discount rate like a central bank. The peg with the foreign currency tends to keep interest rates and inflation very closely aligned to those in the country against whose currency the peg is fixed.

The _____ in question will no longer issue fiat money but instead will only issue one unit of local currency for each unit (or decided amount) of foreign currency it has in its vault (often a hard currency such as the U.S. dollar or the euro.) The surplus on the balance of payments of that country is reflected by higher deposits local banks hold at the central bank as well as (initially) higher deposits of the (net) exporting firms at their local banks.

a. Petrodollar
b. Reserve currency
c. Currency competition
d. Currency board

26. _____ is a fee paid on borrowed assets. It is the price paid for the use of borrowed money, or, money earned by deposited funds. Assets that are sometimes lent with _____ include money, shares, consumer goods through hire purchase, major assets such as aircraft, and even entire factories in finance lease arrangements.

Chapter 15. Into the International Marketplace

a. Internal debt
c. Insolvency
b. Asset protection
d. Interest

27. An _____ is the price a borrower pays for the use of money they do not own, for instance a small company might borrow from a bank to kick start their business, and the return a lender receives for deferring the use of funds, by lending it to the borrower. _____s are normally expressed as a percentage rate over the period of one year.

_____s targets are also a vital tool of monetary policy and are used to control variables like investment, inflation, and unemployment.

a. ACCRA Cost of Living Index
c. Arrow-Debreu model
b. Enterprise value
d. Interest rate

28. _____ is an economic concept, expressed as a basic algebraic identity that relates interest rates and exchange rates. The identity is theoretical, and usually follows from assumptions imposed in economics models. There is evidence to support as well as to refute the concept.
a. Asset specificity
c. Investment protection
b. Ask price
d. Interest rate parity

29. In economics, _____ refers to the ability of a person or a country to produce a particular good at a lower marginal cost and opportunity cost than another person or country. It is the ability to produce a product most efficiently given all the other products that could be produced. It can be contrasted with absolute advantage which refers to the ability of a person or a country to produce a particular good at a lower absolute cost than another.
a. Gravity model of trade
c. Hot money
b. Triffin dilemma
d. Comparative advantage

30. _____ in economics and business is the result of an exchange and from that trade we assign a numerical monetary value to a good, service or asset. If Alice trades Bob 4 apples for an orange, the _____ of an orange is 4 apples. Inversely, the _____ of an apple is 1/4 oranges.
a. Premium pricing
c. Price book
b. Price war
d. Price

31. _____ in economics refers to metrics and measures of output from production processes, per unit of input. Labor _____, for example, is typically measured as a ratio of output per labor-hour, an input. _____ may be conceived of as a metrics of the technical or engineering efficiency of production.
a. Productivity
c. Fordism
b. Piece work
d. Production-possibility frontier

32. _____ is the price of a commodity such as a good or service in terms of another; ie, the ratio of two prices. A _____ may be expressed in terms of a ratio between any two prices or the ratio between the price of one particular good and a weighted average of all other goods available in the market. A _____ is an opportunity cost.
a. False shortage
c. False economy
b. Relative price
d. Food cooperative

33. The _____ is an economic and political union of 27 member states, located primarily in Europe. It was established by the Treaty of Maastricht on 1 November 1993, upon the foundations of the pre-existing European Economic Community. With a population of almost 500 million, the _____ generates an estimated 30% share (US$18.4 trillion in 2008) of the nominal gross world product.
   a. ACEA agreement
   b. ACCRA Cost of Living Index
   c. European Court of Justice
   d. European Union

Chapter 16. Policy Toward Trade

1. _____ is a type of trade policy that allows traders to act and transact without interference from government. Thus, the policy permits trading partners mutual gains from trade, with goods and services produced according to the theory of comparative advantage.

Under a _____ policy, prices are a reflection of true supply and demand, and are the sole determinant of resource allocation.

a. Free Trade
b. 1921 recession
c. 100-year flood
d. 130-30 fund

2. The _____ is a trilateral trade bloc in North America created by the governments of the United States, Canada, and Mexico. The agreement creating the trade bloc came into force on January 1, 1994. It superseded the Canada-United States Free Trade Agreement between the U.S. and Canada.
a. Case-Shiller Home Price Indices
b. North American Free Trade Agreement
c. Federal Reserve Bank Notes
d. Demand-side technologies

3. The _____ was the outcome of the failure of negotiating governments to create the International Trade Organization (ITO.) GATT was formed in 1947 and lasted until 1994, when it was replaced by the World Trade Organization. The Bretton Woods Conference had introduced the idea for an organization to regulate trade as part of a larger plan for economic recovery after World War II.
a. General Agreement on Trade in Services
b. GATT
c. General Agreement on Tariffs and Trade
d. Dutch-Scandinavian Economic Pact

4. In economics, an _____ is any good (e.g. a commodity) or service brought into one country from another country in a legitimate fashion, typically for use in trade.It is a good that is brought in from another country for sale. _____ goods or services are provided to domestic consumers by foreign producers. An _____ in the receiving country is an export to the sending country.
a. Incoterms
b. Import
c. Economic integration
d. Import quota

5. A _____ is a duty imposed on goods when they are moved across a political boundary. They are usually associated with protectionism, the economic policy of restraining trade between nations. For political reasons, _____s are usually imposed on imported goods, although they may also be imposed on exported goods.
a. 100-year flood
b. Tariff
c. 1921 recession
d. 130-30 fund

6. The _____ commenced in September 1986 and continued until April 1994. The round, based on the General Agreement on Tariffs and Trade (GATT) ministerial meeting in Geneva (1982), was launched in Punta del Este in Uruguay (hence the name), followed by negotiations in Montreal, Geneva, Brussels, Washington, D.C., and Tokyo, with the 20 agreements finally being signed in Marrakech - the Marrakesh Agreement. The Round transformed the GATT into the World Trade Organization.
a. AD-IA Model
b. Uruguay round
c. ACCRA Cost of Living Index
d. ACEA agreement

7. _____ in economics and business is the result of an exchange and from that trade we assign a numerical monetary value to a good, service or asset. If Alice trades Bob 4 apples for an orange, the _____ of an orange is 4 apples. Inversely, the _____ of an apple is 1/4 oranges.

Chapter 16. Policy Toward Trade

a. Price war
b. Price
c. Price book
d. Premium pricing

8. In economics, an _____ is any good or commodity, transported from one country to another country in a legitimate fashion, typically for use in trade. _____ goods or services are provided to foreign consumers by domestic producers. _____ is an important part of international trade.

a. Export
b. ACCRA Cost of Living Index
c. AD-IA Model
d. ACEA agreement

9. An autarky is an economy that is self-sufficient and does not take part in international trade, or severely limits trade with the outside world. Likewise the term refers to an ecosystem not affected by influences from the outside, which relies entirely on its own resources. In the economic meaning, it is also referred to as a _____.

a. Transition economy
b. Network Economy
c. Digital economy
d. Closed economy

10. An _____ is an economy in which people, including businesses, can trade in goods and services with other people and businesses in the international community at large. This contrasts with a closed economy in which international trade cannot take place.

The act of selling goods or services to a foreign country is called exporting.

a. Attention work
b. Information economy
c. Indicative planning
d. Open economy

11. The _____ was an act signed into law on June 17, 1930, that raised U.S. tariffs on over 20,000 imported goods to record levels. In the United States 1,028 economists signed a petition against this legislation, and after it was passed, many countries retaliated with their own increased tariffs on U.S. goods, and American exports and imports were reduced by more than half.

Although rated capacity had increased tremendously, actual output, income, and expenditure had not.

a. Loss of use
b. Patent Law Treaty
c. Smoot-Hawley Tariff Act
d. Judgment summons

12. The _____ is an important selective, mainly private, international organization designed by its founders to supervise and liberalize international trade. The organization officially commenced on 1 January 1995, under the Marrakesh Agreement, succeeding the 1947 General Agreement on Tariffs and Trade (GATT.)

The _____ deals with regulation of trade between participating countries; it provides a framework for negotiating and formalising trade agreements, and a dispute resolution process aimed at enforcing participants' adherence to _____ agreements which are signed by representatives of member governments and ratified by their parliaments.

a. Backus-Kehoe-Kydland consumption correlation puzzle
b. World Trade Organization
c. 2009 G-20 London summit protests
d. Bio-energy village

13. _____ are legal property rights over creations of the mind, both artistic and commercial, and the corresponding fields of law. Under _____ law, owners are granted certain exclusive rights to a variety of intangible assets, such as musical, literary, and artistic works; ideas, discoveries and inventions; and words, phrases, symbols, and designs. Common types of _____ include copyrights, trademarks, patents, industrial design rights and trade secrets.

a. Independent contractor
b. Intellectual property
c. Ease of Doing Business Index
d. Expedited Funds Availability Act

14. _____ is a Regional Trade Agreement among Argentina, Brazil, Paraguay and Uruguay founded in 1991 by the Treaty of Asunci>ón, which was later amended and updated by the 1994 Treaty of Ouro Preto. Its purpose is to promote free trade and the fluid movement of goods, people, and currency.

_____ origins trace back to 1985 when Presidents Ra>úl Alfons>ín of Argentina and Jos>é Sarney of Brazil signed the Argentina-Brazil Integration and Economics Cooperation Program or PICE .

a. Mercosur
b. 100-year flood
c. 130-30 fund
d. Free trade area

15. In economics, a _____ may be either a subsidy or a price control, both with the intended effect of keeping the market price of a good higher than the competitive equilibrium level.

In the case of a price control, a _____ is the minimum legal price a seller may charge, typically placed above equilibrium. It is the support of certain price levels at or above market values by the government.

a. Marginal profit
b. Payment schedule
c. Labor intensity
d. Price support

16. A _____ is the exclusive authority to determine how a resource is used, whether that resource is owned by government or by individuals. All economic goods have a _____s attribute. This attribute has three broad components

1. The right to use the good
2. The right to earn income from the good
3. The right to transfer the good to others

The concept of _____s as used by economists and legal scholars are related but distinct. The distinction is largely seen in the economists' focus on the ability of an individual or collective to control the use of the good.

a. High-reeve
b. Holder in due course
c. Post-sale restraint
d. Property right

Chapter 16. Policy Toward Trade

17. Economics:

- _____, the desire to own something and the ability to pay for it
- _____ curve, a graphic representation of a _____ schedule
- _____ deposit, the money in checking accounts
- _____ pull theory, the theory that inflation occurs when _____ for goods and services exceeds existing supplies
- _____ schedule, a table that lists the quantity of a good a person will buy it each different price
- _____ side economics, the school of economics at believes government spending and tax cuts open economy by raising _____

a. Production
b. Variability
c. McKesson ' Robbins scandal
d. Demand

18. The _____ or gross domestic income (GDI), a basic measure of an economy's economic performance, is the market value of all final goods and services produced within the borders of a nation in a year. _____ can be defined in three ways, all of which are conceptually identical. First, it is equal to the total expenditures for all final goods and services produced within the country in a stipulated period of time (usually a 365-day year.)

a. Market structure
b. Monopolistic competition
c. Countercyclical
d. Gross domestic product

19. A _____ is a concept about fairness, not that each player has an equal chance to succeed, but that they all play by the same set of rules. A metaphorical playing field is said to be level if no external interference such as government regulations affects the ability of the players to compete fairly.

Handicapping might be thought of as the opposite concept, of unequal rules designed to make the outcome of play more equal.

a. Classical dichotomy
b. Hedonic treadmill
c. Level playing field
d. Capital levy

20. In economics, _____s are any goods for which demand increases when income increases and falls when income decreases but price remains constant, i.e. with a positive income elasticity of demand. The term does not necessarily refer to the quality of the good.

Depending on the indifference curves, the amount of a good bought can either increase, decrease, or stay the same when income increases.

a. Bord halfpenny
b. Normal good
c. Financial contagion
d. Normative economics

21. A _____ is an object whose consumption increases the utility of the consumer, for which the quantity demanded exceeds the quantity supplied at zero price. _____s are usually modeled as having diminishing marginal utility. The first individual purchase has high utility; the second has less.

| a. Merit good | b. Pie method |
| c. Good | d. Composite good |

22. An _____ is a person who has possession of an enterprise and assumes significant accountability for the inherent risks and the outcome. It is an ambitious leader who combines land, labor, and capital to create and market new goods or services. The term is a loanword from French and was first defined by the Irish economist Richard Cantillon.

| a. Expansionary policies | b. ACEA agreement |
| c. Entrepreneur | d. ACCRA Cost of Living Index |

23. A _____ is a person or investment firm that makes venture investments, and these _____s are expected to bring managerial and technical expertise as well as capital to their investments. A venture capital fund refers to a pooled investment vehicle that primarily invests the financial capital of third-party investors in enterprises that are too risky for the standard capital markets or bank loans.

Venture capital is also associated with job creation, the knowledge economy and used as a proxy measure of innovation within an economic sector or geography.

| a. Club deal | b. Divisional buyout |
| c. Venture capitalist | d. Startup company |

24. _____ are any materials or substances that can be used as fuels, other than conventional fuels. Conventional fuels include: fossil fuels, coal, propane, and natural gas), and nuclear materials such as uranium.

Some well known _____ include biodiesel, bioalcohol, chemically stored electricity, hydrogen, non-fossil methane, non-fossil natural gas, vegetable oil and other biomass sources.

| a. AD-IA Model | b. ACEA agreement |
| c. ACCRA Cost of Living Index | d. Alternative fuels |

25. Many _____ are related to the environmental consequences of production and use

- Systemic risk describes the risks to the overall economy arising from the risks which the banking system takes. That the private costs of banking failure may be smaller than the social costs justifies banking regulations, although regulations could create a moral hazard.

- Anthropogenic climate change is attributed to greenhouse gas emissions from burning oil, gas, and coal. Global warming has been ranked as the #1 externality of all economic activity, in the magnitude of potential harms and yet remains unmitigated.

| a. White certificates | b. Total Economic Value |
| c. Green certificate | d. Negative externalities |

26. Under the system of feudalism, a _____, fief, feud, feoff often consisted of inheritable lands or revenue-producing property granted by a liege lord, generally to a vassal, in return for a form of allegiance, originally to give him the means to fulfill his military duties when called upon. However anything of value could be held in fief, such as an office, a right of exploitation (e.g., hunting, fishing) or any other type of revenue, rather than the land it comes from.

Originally, the feudal institution of vassalage did not imply the giving or receiving of landholdings (which were granted only as a reward for loyalty), but by the eighth century the giving of a landholding was becoming standard.

a. 130-30 fund
c. 1921 recession
b. 100-year flood
d. Fiefdom

Chapter 17. Economic Development

1. _____s is the social science that studies the production, distribution, and consumption of goods and services. The term _____s comes from the Ancient Greek oá¼°κονομῖα from oá¼¶κος (oikos, 'house') + vÏŒμος (nomos, 'custom' or 'law'), hence 'rules of the house(hold)'. Current _____ models developed out of the broader field of political economy in the late 19th century, owing to a desire to use an empirical approach more akin to the physical sciences.
    a. Inflation
    b. Energy economics
    c. Opportunity cost
    d. Economic

2. _____ is the development of economic wealth of countries or regions for the well-being of their inhabitants. It is the process by which a nation improves the economic, political, and social well being of its people. From a policy perspective, _____ can be defined as efforts that seek to improve the economic well-being and quality of life for a community by creating and/or retaining jobs and supporting or growing incomes and the tax base.
    a. Inflation
    b. Experimental economics
    c. Economic methodology
    d. Economic development

3. The _____ is an international organization that oversees the global financial system by following the macroeconomic policies of its member countries, in particular those with an impact on exchange rates and the balance of payments. It is an organization formed to stabilize international exchange rates and facilitate development. It also offers financial and technical assistance to its members, making it an international lender of last resort.
    a. ACEA agreement
    b. Office of Thrift Supervision
    c. ACCRA Cost of Living Index
    d. International Monetary Fund

4. The _____ or gross domestic income (GDI), a basic measure of an economy's economic performance, is the market value of all final goods and services produced within the borders of a nation in a year. _____ can be defined in three ways, all of which are conceptually identical. First, it is equal to the total expenditures for all final goods and services produced within the country in a stipulated period of time (usually a 365-day year.)
    a. Monopolistic competition
    b. Countercyclical
    c. Market structure
    d. Gross domestic product

5. _____ comprises the total value produced within a country (i.e. its gross domestic product), together with its income received from other countries (notably interest and dividends), less similar payments made to other countries.

    The _____ consists of: the personal consumption expenditures, the gross private investment, the government consumption expenditures, the net income from assets abroad (net income receipts), and the gross exports of goods and services, after deducting two components: the gross imports of goods and services, and the indirect business taxes. The _____ is similar to the gross national product (GNP), except that in measuring the GNP one does not deduct the indirect business taxes.

    a. Central limit order book
    b. Base period
    c. Market-based instruments
    d. Gross national income

6. A variety of measures of _____ and output are used in economics to estimate total economic activity in a country or region, including gross domestic product (GDP), gross national product (GNP), and net _____

There are three main ways of calculating these numbers; the output approach, the income approach and the expenditure approach. In theory, the three must yield the same, because total expenditures on goods and services must equal the total income paid to the producers (Gnational income), and that must also equal the total value of the output of goods and services (GNP.)

a. GNI per capita
b. Volume index
c. Gross world product
d. National income

7. The _____ is a derogatory alternative name for economics devised by the Victorian historian Thomas Carlyle in the 19th century. The term is an inversion of the phrase 'gay science,' meaning 'life-enhancing knowledge.' This was a familiar expression at the time, and was later adopted as the title of a book by Nietzsche

It is often stated that Carlyle gave economics the nickname '_____' as a response to the late 18th century writings of The Reverend Thomas Robert Malthus, who grimly predicted that starvation would result as projected population growth exceeded the rate of increase in the food supply.

a. Dismal science
b. 1921 recession
c. 130-30 fund
d. 100-year flood

8. _____ is the change in population over time, and can be quantified as the change in the number of individuals in a population using 'per unit time' for measurement. The term _____ can technically refer to any species, but almost always refers to humans, and it is often used informally for the more specific demographic term _____ rate, and is often used to refer specifically to the growth of the population of the world.

Simple models of _____ include the Malthusian Growth Model and the logistic model.

a. 100-year flood
b. Population dynamics
c. 130-30 fund
d. Population growth

Chapter 17. Economic Development

9. A _____ is:

   - Rewrite _____, in generative grammar and computer science
   - Standardization, a formal and widely-accepted statement, fact, definition, or qualification
   - Operation, a determinate _____ for performing a mathematical operation and obtaining a certain result (Mathematics, Logic)
     - Unary operation
     - Binary operation
   - _____ of inference, a function from sets of formulae to formulae (Mathematics, Logic)
   - _____ of thumb, principle with broad application that is not intended to be strictly accurate or reliable for every situation. Also often simply referred to as a _____
   - Moral, an atomic element of a moral code for guiding choices in human behavior
   - Heuristic, a quantized '_____' which shows a tendency or probability for successful function
   - A regulation, as in sports
   - A Production _____, as in computer science
   - Procedural law, a _____ set governing the application of laws to cases
     - A law, which may informally be called a '_____'
     - A court ruling, a decision by a court
   - In the U.S. Government, a regulation mandated by Congress, but written or expanded upon by the Executive Branch.
   - Norm (sociology), an informal but widely accepted _____, concept, truth, definition, or qualification (social norms, legal norms, coding norms)
   - Norm (philosophy), a kind of sentence or a reason to act, feel or believe
   - 'Rulership' is the concept of governance by a government:
     - Military _____, governance by a military body
     - Monastic _____, a collection of precepts that guides the life of monks or nuns in a religious order where the superior holds the place of Christ
   - Slide _____

   - '_____,' a song by Ayumi Hamasaki
   - '_____,' a song by rapper Nas
   - '_____s,' an album by the band The Whitest Boy Alive
   - _____s: Pyaar Ka Superhit Formula, a 2003 Bollywood film
   - ruler, an instrument for measuring lengths
   - _____, a component of an astrolabe, circumferator or similar instrument
   - The _____s, a bestselling self-help book
   - _____ Project (Run Up-to-date Linux Everywhere), a project that aims to use up-to-date Linux software on old PCs
   - _____ engine, a software system that helps managing business _____s
   - Ja _____, a hip hop artist
     - R.U.L.E., a 2005 greatest hits album by rapper Ja _____
   - '_____s,' a KMFDM song

a. Rule
b. Demand
c. Procter ' Gamble
d. Technocracy

Chapter 17. Economic Development

10. _____ in economics and business is the result of an exchange and from that trade we assign a numerical monetary value to a good, service or asset. If Alice trades Bob 4 apples for an orange, the _____ of an orange is 4 apples. Inversely, the _____ of an apple is 1/4 oranges.
    a. Price war
    b. Price
    c. Price book
    d. Premium pricing

11. A _____ is message sent to consumers and producers in the form of a price charged for a commodity; this is seen as indicating a signal for producers to increase supplies and/or consumers to reduce demand.

    For example, in a free price system, rising prices may indicate a shortage of supply, increase in demand, or a rise in input costs. Regardless of the underlying reason--and without the consumer needing to know the cause--the price increase communicates the notion that consumer demand (at this new, higher price) should recede or that supplies should increase.

    a. Market demand schedule
    b. Price signal
    c. Threshold population
    d. Mohring effect

12. In economics, a _____ is any economic system that effects its distribution of goods and services with prices and employing any form of money or debt tokens. Except for possible remote and primitive communities, all modern societies use _____s to allocate resources. However, _____s are not used for all resource allocation decisions today.
    a. Hanseatic League
    b. Family economy
    c. Neomercantilism
    d. Price system

13. _____ is a situation first proposed by Jagdish Bhagwati, in 1958, where economic growth could result in a country being worse off than before the growth. If growth is heavily export biased it will lead to a fall in the terms of trade of the exporting country, in rare circumstances this fall in the terms of trade may be so large as to outweigh the gains from growth, this situation would cause a country to be worse off after growth than before. This result is only valid if the growing country is able to influence world prices.
    a. Investment-specific technological progress
    b. Austerity
    c. Uneconomic growth
    d. Immiserizing growth

14. A _____ is the exclusive authority to determine how a resource is used, whether that resource is owned by government or by individuals. All economic goods have a _____s attribute. This attribute has three broad components

    1. The right to use the good
    2. The right to earn income from the good
    3. The right to transfer the good to others

    The concept of _____s as used by economists and legal scholars are related but distinct. The distinction is largely seen in the economists' focus on the ability of an individual or collective to control the use of the good.

    a. High-reeve
    b. Post-sale restraint
    c. Property right
    d. Holder in due course

15. The _____ is an international financial institution that provides financial and technical assistance to developing countries for development programs (e.g. bridges, roads, schools, etc.) with the stated goal of reducing poverty.

Chapter 17. Economic Development

The _____ differs from the _____ Group, in that the _____ comprises only two institutions:

- International Bank for Reconstruction and Development (IBRD)
- International Development Association (IDA)

Whereas the latter incorporates these two in addition to three more:

- International Finance Corporation (IFC)
- Multilateral Investment Guarantee Agency (MIGA)
- International Centre for Settlement of Investment Disputes (ICSID)

John Maynard Keynes (right) represented the UK at the conference, and Harry Dexter White represented the US.

The _____ is one of two major financial institutions created as a result of the Bretton Woods Conference in 1944. The International Monetary Fund, a related but separate institution, is the second.

a. Flow to Equity-Approach
c. Bank-State-Branch
b. World Bank
d. Financial costs of the 2003 Iraq War

16. _____ is a voluntary transfer of resources from one country to another, given at least partly with the objective of benefiting the recipient country. It may have other functions as well: it may be given as a signal of diplomatic approval, or to strengthen a military ally, to reward a government for behaviour desired by the donor, to extend the donor's cultural influence, to provide infrastructure needed by the donor for resource extraction from the recipient country, or to gain other kinds of commercial access. Humanitarianism and altruism are, nevertheless, significant motivations for the giving of _____.
  a. Aid
  c. ACCRA Cost of Living Index
  b. ACEA agreement
  d. AD-IA Model

17. A _____ is the transfer of wealth from one party (such as a person or company) to another. A _____ is usually made in exchange for the provision of goods, services or both, or to fulfill a legal obligation.

The simplest and oldest form of _____ is barter, the exchange of one good or service for another.

  a. Going concern
  c. Soft count
  b. Social gravity
  d. Payment

18. Loosely, the _____ is the change in the objective value of the optimal solution of an optimization problem obtained by relaxing the constraint by one unit. In a business application, a _____ is the maximum price that management is willing to pay for an extra unit of a given limited resource. For example, if a production line is already operating at its maximum 40 hour limit, the _____ would be the price of keeping the line operational for an additional hour.
  a. 100-year flood
  c. 130-30 fund
  b. 1921 recession
  d. Shadow price

Chapter 1

1. d	2. c	3. c	4. d	5. b	6. d	7. d	8. d	9. c	10. b
11. a	12. b	13. c	14. b	15. b	16. b	17. d	18. d	19. c	20. a
21. d	22. c	23. d	24. b	25. d	26. b	27. d	28. b	29. d	30. c
31. d	32. d	33. d	34. d	35. a	36. d	37. d	38. d	39. c	

Chapter 2

1. a	2. d	3. a	4. d	5. d	6. a	7. d	8. d	9. b	10. d
11. d	12. c	13. b	14. d	15. a	16. d	17. d	18. c	19. d	20. d
21. a	22. d	23. c							

Chapter 3

| 1. b | 2. b | 3. b | 4. a | 5. d | 6. a | 7. d | 8. d | 9. d | 10. d |
| 11. d | 12. d | 13. a | 14. d | 15. c | | | | | |

Chapter 4

1. d	2. a	3. d	4. b	5. b	6. d	7. d	8. d	9. d	10. d
11. b	12. a	13. a	14. d	15. a	16. c	17. b	18. d	19. d	20. a
21. a	22. a	23. d	24. d	25. a	26. a	27. d			

Chapter 5

1. c	2. c	3. d	4. d	5. d	6. c	7. b	8. d	9. d	10. d
11. d	12. d	13. b	14. c	15. d	16. d	17. d	18. c	19. c	20. d
21. d	22. d	23. a	24. d	25. d	26. c	27. b	28. d	29. b	30. d
31. b	32. d	33. d	34. a	35. d	36. d	37. d	38. d	39. b	40. b
41. d	42. d	43. d	44. d	45. d	46. d	47. c	48. d	49. b	50. d
51. d	52. d	53. b	54. d	55. d	56. c				

Chapter 6

| 1. d | 2. b | 3. d | 4. a | 5. d | 6. a | 7. d | 8. c | 9. b | 10. d |
| 11. d | 12. a | 13. d | 14. d | 15. d | 16. d | | | | |

Chapter 7

1. a	2. b	3. d	4. a	5. b	6. d	7. b	8. d	9. c	10. d
11. d	12. b	13. c	14. b	15. d	16. d	17. c	18. c	19. d	20. d
21. a	22. d	23. c	24. a	25. c	26. d	27. d	28. d	29. d	30. d
31. a	32. d	33. c	34. d						

Chapter 8

1. d	2. d	3. d	4. a	5. c	6. d	7. b	8. d	9. d	10. d
11. b	12. c	13. b	14. a	15. c	16. d	17. a	18. d	19. d	20. d
21. d	22. b	23. c	24. c	25. b	26. a	27. d	28. d	29. d	

ANSWER KEY

Chapter 9
1. d   2. d   3. c   4. b   5. d   6. d   7. d   8. d   9. d   10. d
11. a   12. d   13. b   14. d   15. d   16. b   17. b   18. d   19. a   20. b
21. d   22. b   23. c   24. b   25. b   26. b   27. d   28. c   29. a   30. a
31. d   32. c   33. a   34. a

Chapter 10
1. d   2. d   3. d   4. d   5. b   6. d   7. d   8. d   9. d   10. d
11. a   12. b   13. b   14. d   15. d   16. c   17. d   18. a   19. c   20. b
21. a   22. c   23. d   24. d   25. b   26. a   27. b   28. c   29. a

Chapter 11
1. c   2. c   3. c   4. d   5. d   6. a   7. a   8. d   9. d   10. d
11. c   12. c   13. d   14. c   15. a   16. d   17. d   18. a   19. d   20. c
21. a   22. a   23. d   24. d   25. d   26. d   27. d   28. b   29. b   30. c
31. a   32. c

Chapter 12
1. d   2. d   3. d   4. b   5. d   6. d   7. d   8. d   9. d   10. a
11. a   12. d   13. b   14. b   15. a   16. d   17. d   18. d   19. c   20. d

Chapter 13
1. d   2. d   3. a   4. b   5. b   6. d   7. d   8. c   9. d   10. d
11. d   12. d   13. c   14. a   15. d   16. b   17. d   18. d   19. d   20. d
21. d   22. c   23. c   24. d   25. b   26. d   27. b   28. d   29. d   30. b
31. d   32. a   33. b   34. a   35. d   36. d   37. d   38. d   39. d   40. a
41. a   42. a   43. d   44. d   45. d   46. a   47. b   48. d

Chapter 14
1. c   2. a   3. c   4. d   5. c   6. d   7. d   8. b   9. d   10. d
11. d   12. d   13. d   14. d   15. a   16. d   17. b   18. c   19. d   20. a
21. c   22. d   23. d   24. d   25. d   26. d   27. a   28. d   29. b   30. c
31. b   32. c   33. b

Chapter 15
1. d   2. d   3. d   4. d   5. d   6. d   7. d   8. a   9. a   10. d
11. d   12. c   13. a   14. a   15. d   16. d   17. c   18. d   19. c   20. d
21. a   22. d   23. d   24. d   25. d   26. d   27. d   28. d   29. d   30. d
31. a   32. b   33. d

Chapter 16
1. a   2. b   3. c   4. b   5. b   6. b   7. b   8. a   9. d   10. d
11. c   12. b   13. b   14. a   15. d   16. d   17. d   18. d   19. c   20. b
21. c   22. c   23. c   24. d   25. d   26. d

Chapter 17
1. d 2. d 3. d 4. d 5. d 6. d 7. a 8. d 9. a 10. b
11. b 12. d 13. d 14. c 15. b 16. a 17. d 18. d

www.ingramcontent.com/pod-product-compliance
Lightning Source LLC
Chambersburg PA
CBHW082049230426
43670CB00016B/2835